How to Get Out of Debt: Get an "A" Credit Rating for Free Using the System I've Used Successfully With Thousands of Clients

by Harrine Freeman

How to Get Out of Debt:
Get an "A" Credit Rating for Free Using the System I've Used Successfully With Thousands of Clients

by Harrine Freeman

Adept Publishers
Washington, DC

Adept Publishers books are available at special quantity discounts. Contact the Sales Manager at:

Adept Publishers
P.O. Box 60851
Washington, DC 20039
866-550-7866 (office)
sales@adeptpublishers.com

Library of Congress Catalog Number

Freeman, Harrine.
How to get out of debt: get an "A" credit rating for free using the system I've used successfully with thousands of clients/ by Harrine Freeman.
p. cm.

Includes bibliographical references and index.
ISBN 1–933949–43–0
1. Self Help – United States. 2. Business and Economics/Personal Finance – United States.

2006904756

10 9 8 7 6 5 4 3 2

Cover by Keith Sanders, mariondesigns.com

Acknowledgments

I would like to acknowledge the following people for inspiring me to write this book, Judine Slaughter, Taundra Hayes, Noriko Reid, Norman Turner, all of my family, friends, and others who have always supported me. I also want to thank my editor Lisa Tener for her excellent work, advice and support.

Contents

How I Got Out of Debt

Is a cloud of debt hanging over your head, limiting your ability to live your life? Are you beginning to feel that your debt is affecting how people see you? Affecting your eligibility for jobs? You are not alone. According to the Fair Isaac Corporation (FICO) approximately 30 million Americans are in debt and receive bad credit ratings every year. A high risk credit score is a score below approximately 620 (on average and depending on the lender) which means scores at this level usually get denied when applying for credit. Over a million Americans file for bankruptcy every year. One in every 73 households files for bankruptcy. In 2005, 2 million Americans filed for personal bankruptcies.

Unfortunately, debt stops you from achieving your goals and dreams. It prevents you from saving and destroys your credit. Debt causes creditors, employers and employees to believe that you are not a trustworthy person. You could pay someone hundreds of dollars to fix your credit by going to a credit counseling agency or an individual who promises they can fix your credit, but instead you have this book, which is a lot cheaper and puts you in the driver's seat.

So why not use this book instead to help you do it on your own, like I did. People who know me know find it hard to believe, but I was deeply in debt once. Like you, I've been there. I don't know what my credit score was but let's just say that my credit was bad (luckily I was still living at home). Since becoming debt free myself, I have made a great living helping thousands of people like you eliminate their debt and achieve an "A" credit rating.

Can you imagine how your life would change if you had good credit? Imagine the relief – less stress, not worrying about bill collectors calling you at home or at work, and putting an end to your fights with your partner, spouse or children that are caused by not having any money. You would be able to buy things that you needed or wanted, and get a good interest rate for a home or car loan. These are just some of the many benefits of having good credit and using this book can help you get that good credit.

My own story begins my sophomore year in college. Every day as I walked to class I passed three or four tables where vendors urged students to fill out a simple credit card application bribing us with a free t–shirt, mug, water bottle, hat or key chain. All you had to do was be approved for a credit card. Even the free key chain was enough motivation for me. I didn't realize what I was getting into. Approval came quickly since I had no credit. They didn't seem to mind that I also had no job.

When my first credit card arrived in the mail, all I could think about was my free t-shirt and how I could buy whatever I wanted. My shopping sprees began with a day at Lerner's and the Limited. I bought a pink sweater, two button up shirts, two pairs of jeans, a cute leather purse, and three pairs of shoes. I floated on cloud 9 all day. And I didn't have to do anything to make these purchases–like work or earn money. I just handed the sales clerk a small piece of plastic and–bingo–everything was mine to keep.

My next spree occurred in a candle shop. I bought all kinds of candles—aromatherapy candles, romantic candles, two candles of each kind and color, tall skinny candles, big fat candles, candles with one wick, candles with three wicks and, of course, candle holders for each candle. I felt so free to buy things without having to worry about asking my mother for the money.

Within in three years I owned thirteen credit cards – Visa, Discover, two gas cards (although I had no driver's license or car), two Hecht's cards, and joint credit cards with my friends whom I let use my credit cards (big mistake).

Also, I let family members use my credit cards – another big mistake since they never paid the bill. The unpaid bills were eventually reported on my credit report. I even used the gas cards to buy my friends gas when we went places (another big mistake). I was completely out of control, but having fun.

Finally my mother realized what was going on and took the credit cards from me. That didn't work; I just found her hiding place and continued to charge. Next, she sat me down and said that I needed to stop charging because I was in school and didn't have a job and she couldn't pay back my debt. I agreed that I had a problem and began cutting up my credit cards but, by this time, I was $10,000 in debt.

I began paying the minimum monthly payment on each credit card, which got me nowhere. Credit card companies calculate a minimum payment due that could keep you in debt forever. Things really went downhill when I moved out on my own. After about six months I lost my job and my credit got even worse, I owed over $11,000. Credit card companies were calling my home day and night, being very rude and nasty, and threatening me.

The icing on the cake was the car I bought in my name for my boyfriend who agreed to pay the car note each month. That lasted for about six months, after which I received a notice saying that payments had not been made for two months. When he stopped making payments altogether, the car company tried to repossess the car.

He hid the car and the car company came to my job and threatened to take me to jail if I did not tell them where the car was. I was still with my boyfriend – that's another topic. I told him what they said and he reassured me that they could not take me to jail and that they were threatening me. They finally left my workplace, found the car and repossessed it. I ended up owing them $9,000 dollars on top of the $11,000 that I already owed.

I finally decided that I needed to put myself on a budget. I brought my lunch to work every day for one year. I set up a payment plan and paid the minimum monthly payment each month. I set up a payment plan with the car company for the repossession, which had also been reported to a collection agency.

I also realized that I needed additional money to pay these bills, because I was not getting anywhere. To supplement my somewhat meager salary, I found a part–time job and used that money to pay my debt down. A relative offered to pay one of my credit card bills for about $1,000. I worked a full–time job and a part–time job for one year. By the end of the year I saw results and had paid down some of my debt. However, the entire process to become completely debt free took four years.

I negotiated with the companies and asked them what I could do to restore my credit, explaining the circumstances of the repossession, the family member using my credit card and friends borrowing my credit cards. I got in a conversation with one representative from a credit card company who offered some good advice. He told me to write letters to the credit card companies explaining my situation, offering to set up payment plans, and then to negotiate with them.

His advice worked. I have been debt free for the past ten years. Once I became debt free I began offering advice to my friends and have been ever since. I purchased a car and a home, paid off my car and now only have a mortgage payment. Five years later my friend encouraged me to become a credit counselor, and so I did.

Be cautious before going to a credit repair counseling agency or bankruptcy lawyer to help repair your credit. They promise to erase all your debts and make you believe you will have good credit after using their services. They do not do anything special that you cannot do for yourself. They simply take the time to analyze the situation and call or write letters to get the matter resolved.

Based on my personal experiences with debt, and after helping thousands of clients, I wrote the following chapters to teach you how to be debt free, whether you're single, divorced, widowed, married, separated, unemployed, underemployed, a college student, whatever your specific situation is, and tell you how to do it on your own, so you don't incur more debt hiring someone to do it for you!

Chapter 1 – Do You Have the Warning Signs of Bad Credit?

How bad is your credit? How has your bad credit affected you and your life? Your credit history is a critical element of your financial life. It contains information that can affect many areas of your life. Your credit history can be viewed by potential creditors, potential employers, employers, state and local government agencies, potential insurance companies, potential investors and lenders. Your credit history develops from taking personal information you provide on credit applications such as your name, social security number, age, address, previous address, telephone number, current and previous employers and date of birth.

Here are five warning signs of bad credit:

- You have account balances at or above 50% of the limit.
- You have more than 3 accounts with balances (if you have more than 3 accounts try to reduce the number of accounts down to 3).
- You have a minimum of 2 accounts with $1,000 limit (this can vary based on your income).
- You pay for everything with a credit card.
- You constantly make late payments on your accounts.

If you neglect to pay your bills on time, or don't pay your bills at all, you develop a negative credit history and are viewed as a credit risk. You must first recognize that you have poor credit and then take steps to improve your credit rating. Your credit history did not turn from good to bad overnight and improving your credit rating will not happen overnight either. Before you begin developing a plan for improving your credit rating, or before making a purchase, you must first determine if you have credit problems. You should always save money no matter what your financial situation.

Your credit report contains information such as: names of creditors, account or loan number, current balance, high limit, credit limit, monthly payment amount, type of account (installment, revolving, or mortgage), account category (joint, individual, authorized user), date the account was opened and/or closed, payment history and the date information was last reported.

The inquiries section of your credit report lists creditors and other companies who checked your credit history. Some inquiries are screened to provide credit offers (pre–approvals for credit), some for monitoring your account and some for reviewing your account for various reasons such as increasing a credit limit or canceling an account. Inquiries that affect your credit score are: inquiries for new accounts opened, number of recent inquiries, time since the recent account opening and the type of account, and the time since the credit inquiry.

For example if you applied for a credit card on 1/16/2006 and applied for another credit card on 2/22/2006 this is a red flag to lenders whether you were approved or not because lenders assume that you were denied credit or believe you have poor spending habits applying for two credit card accounts so close together. If you open a new account wait at least six months before applying for another account.

Depending on your credit score one additional inquiry may affect your score by 5 points or more, or may not affect your score at all. If you have six or more inquiries on your credit report you are considered a high risk and are perceived to be a possible candidate to apply for bankruptcy. If you are shopping around for the best deal when buying a car or home inquiries that are obtained within a 14 day period are usually counted as one inquiry but this also depends on the company reviewing your credit report. If your credit report has inquiries for a car or mortgage loan within 30 days prior to getting your credit score the inquiries may not affect your score. Past due bills, public records, and collections can seriously hurt your credit.

Your credit score is the figure most lenders use to approve you for loans, credit cards and financing. Most people with credit have a credit score between 300 and 650. The range for a credit score is 300 to 850 with 850 being the highest score. The higher your credit score, the more likely a lender will view your application for credit. For example, a credit score of 650 is below average. This leads lenders to believe that you are more likely to become delinquent on one or more accounts. The credit score is not always the only criterion on which your credit application is scored. However, some creditors will approve you for credit, but your interest rate will be higher and you might you have to pay up front fees, since you are considered a high risk.

A new credit score will be used called the Vantage Score which will range from 501 to 990 and correspond to letter grades with "A" credit ranging from 901–990 and "F" credit ranging from 501–600. The lender pays the credit bureau (credit reporting) agency for the credit score. The credit bureau agency pays the Fair Isaac Corporation (FICO) to use the credit score. The Vantage score is being developed by the credit bureau agencies so they don't have to use the FICO score. However, lenders prefer using the FICO score. The Vantage score is currently available to customers for a nominal fee and can be ordered by calling the three major credit reporting agencies, Experian, TransUnion and Equifax. This new score will cause many people who currently have excellent or good credit to be categorized as having good or average credit, so it is even more important that you repair your credit as soon as possible.

Here are six tips when considering applying for credit:

- Get a copy of your credit report and review it before applying for credit to ensure you get the best rate.
- Shop around for the best interest rates; check out www.bankrate.com for rate comparisons.
- Don't apply for department store or gas cards because the interest rates are higher than the average rates.
- If you apply for credit and are denied, don't apply again for at least six months.
- Don't apply for credit just because you see a store having a sale and they offer 10% off of your purchase. You won't even see that 10% when you get your credit card bill.
- Don't apply for joint accounts unless you are married.

Carrying balances on too many credit accounts at once is an indicator of future delinquencies. For credit cards, even if you pay off your balance in full every month, your credit report may still show a balance on those cards. The total balance on your current statement or previous statement is generally the amount that will show on your credit report. In order to improve your credit score, pay down the balances on all your credit obligations. For revolving accounts, once they are paid down, keep your balances low. Consolidating your debt by transferring balances from many accounts to fewer accounts will not necessarily raise your score, because the same total amount is still owed.

Evaluation of your level of revolving debt is one of the most important factors in a credit score. The credit score evaluates your total balances in relation to your total available credit on revolving accounts, as well as on individual revolving accounts. Installment accounts (non–revolving) are indicated on your credit report as I1, I2, through I9, I9 being a repossession or collection. Installment accounts are: for a given amount of credit available such as a car or loan. A greater amount owed indicates a greater risk, and lowers your credit score. Revolving accounts are a fixed amount of credit that is expected not to be exceeded and a set amount is anticipated to be repaid every month for accounts such as credit cards that are indicated on your credit report as R1, R2 through R9. Mortgage accounts are indicated on your credit report as M1, M2 through M9, M9 being a foreclosure on a home. The ratings range from 0 or 1 to 9. Any rating above 1 is considered negative and indicates that you have made at least one late payment on a particular account.

Paying down your revolving account balances is a good sign that you are able and willing to manage and repay your debt, and this will increase your credit score. Shifting balances among revolving accounts, opening up new revolving accounts, and closing other revolving accounts will not improve your score, and could possibly decrease your score and you will be considered a risk. Depending on the statute of limitations in your state if you have an account that is several years old but not seven years old and you start making payments or pay the account off, the creditor may update the date of last activity to the date the last payment was made. Find out about the statute of limitations in your state regarding debt before making a payment to ensure your account is properly updated.

Refer to Appendix D for more information. For example, if you have a bill that is six years old and have not made any payments on the account it might be better to not make any payments on the account and wait the seven years for the account to be removed from your credit report. However, if the company has contacted you within this time period requesting payment it is best to make a payment or offer a settlement to reduce the chances of your wages being garnished or having a judgment filed against you. This is explained in more detail in Chapter 3.

Some lenders may view consumers with a credit score of 670 as a slightly high risk. Different lenders will evaluate other factors besides the credit score in their review of a loan application. While there are many lenders who might approve loan applicants with a credit score of 670, they may do so with higher rates or more restrictive terms. Paying down your revolving account balances will increase your credit score. Your score is likely to improve as your credit history ages. Paying off your debt on one or more accounts can also raise your credit score.

There are several factors that are used to evaluate your credit score such as: payment history, length of credit history, new credit, the types of credit you have, and the amount of debt owed. Payment history tracks whether you have made payments on time. Length of credit history tracks how long you have had credit for each open account. New credit tracks how many new accounts you have opened and if these new accounts cause your debt–to–income–ratio (debt–ratio) to be over 28%.

The types of credit you have tracks the type of credit accounts you have such as credit card, installment accounts, mortgage loans, etc. The amount of debt owed tracks your outstanding debt (any debt you currently owe) and whether the balance is near the credit limit. Your payment history and the amount of debt owed are the two biggest factors in determining your credit score. However, there are other factors that affect your credit score that each lender uses which are too many to list here but some of them are: length at residence, length of employment, salary and total debt owed.

Sometimes credit card companies give you a limit, say $500, then six months later you get your statement and see that your limit has increased to $1000. This is because the credit card company sees that you pay your bills on time and do not appear to be a high risk so they increase your limit without your permission in hopes that you will use more credit, and even charge the entire limit, thereby making them more money. I experienced the same thing myself; my limit was increased three times by $500 each time. If this happens to you, immediately call your credit card company and tell them to decrease your limit to the original amount. This will keep you disciplined and prevent you from going on shopping sprees.

Here are six tips to help you improve your score over time:

- Apply for credit only when you need it.
- Pay for everything with cash and use your credit card for emergencies only.
- Try to keep steady employment by remaining at a job for at

least two years.

- Try to remain at your residence for at least two years.
- Pay off all old balances.
- Get current on all newer balances.

Consumers who apply for several new credit accounts are at a much greater risk than consumers not seeking credit. This occurs when your credit report contains too many inquiries posted as a result of applying for credit. Inquiries are the only information lenders have that indicates a consumer is actively seeking credit. A common myth is that every single inquiry that appears on your credit report will decrease your credit score a certain number of points. There are different types of inquiries that reside on your credit report. The credit score only considers those inquiries that were posted as a result of you applying for credit. Other types of inquiries, such as promotional inquiries (where a lender has pre–approved you for a credit offer) or consumer disclosure inquiries (where you have requested a copy of your own report) are not considered in the credit score.

The only inquiries that affect your credit score are inquiries where a company checks your credit report to approve you for a car, home, loan, credit card, etc. Promotional inquiries do not count against your credit score and are obtained to offer goods or services or extend a line of credit such as pre–approved credit cards. The impact of inquiries on your credit score will vary depending on your overall credit profile. Inquiries will usually have a larger impact on a credit score for consumers with a limited credit history and on consumers with previous late payment behavior. Also, if you apply for a credit card one month and then apply for a credit card again a few months later both inquiries will appear on your credit report. This is viewed negatively by lenders because they are trying to figure out why someone needs to apply for credit several times in a short amount of time. Inquiries are generally removed from your credit report after two years.

The first step to determine if you have bad credit is to do an analysis of your financial situation. What are your spending habits? How do you pay for your purchases? Are you harassed by creditors at home or at work? Do you always borrow money, get cash advances or live above your means? These are things to think about when trying to determine if you have bad credit. Don't be overwhelmed by the tips in this chapter. It may take some time to make these tips a regular habit. Prioritize the tips you want to do first and then work towards using all of them. The first step to accomplishing anything is to admit you have a problem and then develop a plan to eliminate or overcome that problem. If you find that you have bad credit based on the information in this chapter, don't be scared. You are not alone and you can fix this problem. It requires discipline and time. I know you can do it just like I did!

Chapter 2 – How to Create Your Own Reasonable Spending Plan

Now that you have determined that you have credit problems and you have the information you need to prevent your credit from getting worse, there are several things you can do to repair your credit and begin trying to eliminate your debt. The first step is to create a spending plan (budget). You can refer to Appendices B and C for sample budget worksheets. If I had not created a budget and mapped out my all of my bills I would have never been able to pay my debt off as quickly as I did. Creating a budget also allowed me to set goals, achieve them and build confidence in knowing that I could repair my credit and eventually become debt free.

A budget will help you identify what your expenses are and what your assets are, if any. Creating a budget clearly identifies how your money is spent each month, and over an extended period of time. A budget also helps you to create financial goals and will help you eliminate your debts.

I created a budget for myself. As I mentioned earlier, I packed my lunch every day for a year. In addition, I ate breakfast at home and didn't go out to eat at all. I cancelled my cable service and my pager service. I didn't buy any new clothes and wore the same pair of shoes (they were red) for six months. I sat down and figured out how much money I had and how much I owed. I prioritized my bills from the most owed to the least owed. I set up payment plans with some of the creditors and cut up all of my credit cards. You may not have to do this, but I had to because I had no discipline and would have kept on charging on my credit cards.

I closed all of my department stores cards, Hecht's and Nordstrom, because the interest rates were too high. I negotiated a written agreement from each creditor for all of the payment plans I had set up and slowly began paying off each debt. I also found a part–time job and worked two jobs for one year. After that year I had paid all of my small debts. Then I began tackling my large debts, such as the car repossession and other credit cards with large balances. I could see that my sacrifices were paying off and that, even though I got myself into this mess, I had what it takes to get myself out.

You can begin the first step to creating a spending plan by opening a savings account and checking account. Save, save, save. Save as much money as you can, even if you save a dollar a week or a dollar a month. That is a start. Research at least five banks in your area to find out what restrictions apply to savings accounts, the interest rate and the minimum amount needed to open a savings account. By doing this you will find which bank will provide the best options for your financial needs. Also, keep track of all money going in and coming out – keep track of all of your bills and of how much money you earn.

Open a retirement account. If your job has a thrift savings plan, 401(k) or retirement plan, invest as much as possible but do not put a financial burden on yourself. The minimum you can invest in a 401(k) is approximately 1% of each paycheck. If you are completely overwhelmed with debt, talk to your benefits representative to find out when the enrollment season begins for joining your company 401(k) or retirement plan. Then you can set financial goals to pay off some of your debts and, when enrollment season becomes available, you will be in a better financial position to participate.

Invest your money. Investing your money is the first step to becoming financially independent and gaining assets. If you are not knowledgeable about how to invest your money, contact a financial advisor in your area and inquire about the different options available to you such as mutual funds, stocks, bonds, certificate of deposits (CD's), etc. You can also gain assets by purchasing a home or other real estate.

Call your local bank and inquire about opening a money market account. These usually have a better interest rate than regular savings accounts. Some banks offer an option that allows you to invest the money in your money market account and access it easily at any time with little or no fees.

Depending on your salary, you may not have enough saved to support yourself during retirement. Depending on your age, Social Security may not be available for you when you retire. Many people think of their life in terms of day to day living, never thinking about their future or planning for retirement. This is more important today than ever before. When you reach retirement age you will probably need an additional source of income other than Social Security, if you are lucky enough to receive any Social Security.

Even if you are near retirement age, you can still begin saving. **Call a local brokerage firm or talk to a financial advisor about the various options available to you, and what your immediate financial goals and needs are for the future.**

If you have never saved money before, set goals for yourself and reward yourself by buying yourself something inexpensive (don't go back into debt buying yourself something expensive like jewelry or designer clothing – buy something with cash that is under $15, and don't use your credit card) when you achieve a few of your goals. As you change your way of thinking about money, you will find your lifestyle changing accordingly.

I wish someone had told me how important credit is in life. I wish I had understood the value of money when I was younger. I never would have charged and borrowed so much.

Luckily your credit can be repaired but it takes time, just as it took time to mess it up. Repairing your credit can take as little as one month and as long as several years. There is no quick way to repair your credit, although many companies claim that this is possible and provide guarantees that your credit can be repaired quickly.

Working every day, we are so consumed with life and forget to pay ourselves. Pay yourself first even if it is only $1. Then pay everyone else (bills, creditors, etc.). This means putting money into your savings account and that will continue to grow with each deposit you make. Eventually you will have $100 saved, then $200, then $1000. Keep saving until you have enough to pay at least six months worth of bills. Don't get discouraged if it takes a long time to reach this point. Just stay encouraged that you are saving and continue to inspire yourself each time you read your monthly bank statements.

Purchase items with a debit card, bank check card or cash. Reduce your use of your ATM card. Try to limit your use to three times a month. Check with several banks in your area to find the best type of bank check card for you.

Accounts that offer free checking and free ATM use will limit your fees and be a wiser choice. Debit and check cards are great ways to make purchases without getting into debt. Be sure to read the terms of your debit and check cards in the event that you purchase more than the amount of money that is in your account. You'll need to be disciplined and balance your checkbook every day.

If you are in debt you can save money by reducing your expenses. **Here are twenty tips to help reduce expenses:**

— Pack your lunch for work every day.

— Buy drinks from the grocery store instead of the newsstand at work or coffee shop or, better yet, drink water – it's the best thing for your health and it's free. Reduce all unnecessary spending (i.e. only buy necessary items).

— Use direct deposit to send your paycheck directly to your bank.

— If you get a raise, save all or most of the money received from the raise. For example, save $5 or $10 a week or whatever you can afford. Set a goal that you want to save $100 within a certain time period. Once you have accomplished that goal, set another savings goal and continue doing that. The next time you meet your goal, you will realize that you have saved a great deal.

— Buy what you can on sale, instead of paying the regular price.

— Use coupons or shop at a wholesale store such as Sam's Club or Costco.

— Buy whole foods, such as vegetables, grains, beans and fruits, instead of processed foods. This way you aren't paying for the processing costs.

— Check your local health food store to see if you can buy foods, such as grains, seeds, nuts, spices and legumes, in bulk. This way you aren't paying for expensive packaging.

— Carpool.

— Take public transportation to work.

— Cancel your cable service or get the cheapest plan possible.

— Cancel your cell phone service or get the cheapest plan possible.

— Reduce the amount of long–distance calls you make per month.

— Shop around with various banks to find a checking account with no monthly fees.

— Buy a midsize or compact car until your debts are paid, because this results in a cheaper monthly payment.

— Finds ways to reduce home expenses by buying energy efficient appliances, ceiling fans, programmable thermostats, fluorescent light bulbs and lamps, or hot water insulator jackets.

— Donate items not being used to a charity. The amount can be written off on your taxes.

— Rent movies instead of going to the movie theater.

— Turn the lights out when you are not in a room.

— Turn the heat and/or air conditioner off when you are not at home or set at a low energy saving temperature which can be found be calling your local utility company.

Set several financial goals: for example, one to pay off your debts and one to save money. To do this you must prioritize your bills and decide which debts will be paid first. If you have several debts and have to make monthly payments on each one, here is an example of how to pay each bill until a bill has been completely paid in full. For example, if your financial picture is as follows:

— Total Debt = $5,000

— Savings = 0

— Bi–weekly income (after taxes) = $1,000

— Monthly Expenses = $850

— Debt1 – Visa – $700 (minimum payment $20 a month)

— Debt2 – Student Loan – $3,000 (minimum payment $70 a month)

— Debt3 – Medical Bills – $1,000

— Debt4 – Department Store Credit Card $300 (minimum payment $20 a month).

Total – You have $1,150 (1000 + 1000 – 850) left each month to pay your debts.

Make a list of all your bills and prioritize them based on interest rate and balance. Choose the bill that has the lowest balance and highest interest rate and then send a monthly amount greater than the minimum payment until that bill is paid. Once the bill is paid, check the interest rate, if it is above 11% close the account and cancel the card because you will be paying too much money in interest and finance charges.

If all of your credit cards have an 11% interest rate or higher do research to find new credit cards with a cheaper interest rate or negotiate with your creditors to reduce the interest rate. As your credit score increases you can negotiate for a lower interest rate. Also send the minimum monthly payment for the other bills each month if possible. If this becomes difficult to do on your current salary, consider getting a part–time job to help with paying your debts.

In this example:
— Send $700 to pay off your Visa bill.
— Send the minimum payment amount ($70) for your student loan.
— Send $30 each month towards your medical bills.
— Send $300 to pay off the Department store bill.

— Put at least $50 a month in a savings account.

You would have $1,150 – $300 (Department store) = $850 left. $850 – $700 (Visa) = $150 left. $150 – $30 (medical bills) = $120 left. $120 – $70 (student loan) = $50 left. The remaining $50 is put into a savings account. In one month you were able to pay off the Department Store and Visa bills plus put money away in a savings account. Total Debt Paid = $700 + $70 + $30 + $300 = $1,100. Your total debt now is $3,900 ($5,000 – $1,100).

The next month, you can pay $465 towards your student loan, $485 towards your medical bills, and $200 in a savings account. Your total debt now is $2,950 ($3,900 – $465 – $485). In two months you have reduced your total debt from $5,000 to $2,950 and have saved $250 ($200 + $50). Pay the same amount the next month and you will have paid off your medical bills ($485 + $485 + $30 = $1,000). In three months you have reduced your total debt from $5,000 to $2,000 ($2,950 – $465 – $485). In the fourth month pay $1,000 to your student loan (the money that you were paying towards your medical bills plus a little extra ($485 + $465 + $50 = $1,000) and put $150 in your savings account. In four months you saved $600 ($50 + $200 + $200 + $150). You have also paid $2,000 ($70+ $465 + $465 + $1,000) towards your student loan and now owe $1,000. Do this again next month and your student loan will be paid and put $150 in your savings account. Talk to your benefits representative about putting money in your company's 401(K) or retirement plan. You can also talk to a financial advisor to determine your short–term and long–term financial goals and how best to distribute your money.

If you are unable to pay your bills by check due to bounced checks or bad credit, pay them with money orders until you are able to open a checking account. Create a budget for yourself and stick to it until all your debts are paid off. Create a list of your monthly expenses to evaluate how much you owe. Find out the conditions for late payments, over the limit charges and what the minimum payments are for each creditor. Let's use Mary as an example. Mary earns $1,000 every two weeks after taxes. She has no savings or retirement. Below is list of Mary's monthly expenses.

Type of Bill	Monthly Payment	Interest Rate	Balance Due
Visa	$ 30	19.98%	$ 1,000
Student Loan	$ 70	9 %	$ 3,500
Macy's	$ 30	21.95%	$ 1,200
MasterCard	$ 35	21.95%	$ 500
Car Payment	$ 350	5.9 %	$12,000
Rent (Apt.)	$ 800	———-	———
Rental Ins. (Apt.)	$ 50	———	———
Car Ins.	$ 70	———	———
Phone Bill	$ 30	———	———
Cable Bill	$ 55	———	———
Cell Phone Bill	$ 29	———	———
Pager Bill	$ 12	———	———
Misc. Expenses	$ 200	———	———
Totals	$1,861	———	$19,220

Table 1 – Mary's Monthly Expenses

Mary's total monthly expenses are $1,861. Mary has an additional $139 a month after paying her expenses ($2,000 per month income, $1,861 in bills: $2,000 – $1,861 = $139). If I was counseling Mary, and you were Mary, I would tell her that her first step is to cancel her cable service. This reduces monthly her expenses by $55. Next, cancel her pager service. This reduces her monthly expenses by an additional $12. She has just reduced her total monthly expenses by $67. Next, I would tell her to cancel her cellular phone service. If she absolutely must have a cellular phone, get a prepaid cellular phone in case of emergencies or get the cheapest plan available. The cheapest plans available usually start off at $19.99 a month. This will reduce her monthly expenses by another $10 ($29 – $19.99). Mary has just reduced her expenses by $77 ($55 + $12 + $10).

Now Mary has an additional $216 ($139 + $77) a month after to use toward paying her bills. Mary can pay $130 towards her MasterCard bill and can put $86 in her savings account. Mary has just made her first accomplishment towards getting out of debt. Mary now owes $370 ($500 – $130) on her MasterCard bill. Her total debt is now $19,090 ($19,220 – $130).

If you have a good driving record, shop around for the best insurance rate. You may be able to reduce your car insurance payments. Also, shop around for a lower interest rate for your Visa or MasterCard credit cards. You can transfer your balances to the lower interest rate credit cards because you will end up paying less in interest and the total amount owed will be reduced. Credit unions usually have lower interest rates for credit cards. Make sure you read the agreement that comes along with the credit card regarding the low interest rate. There are usually certain terms and conditions to keep the low interest rate.

Try to avoid paying just the minimum monthly payment on your credit cards. If you continue to pay only the minimum monthly payment you will end up paying 3 times what you actually charged due to the interest that accrues on your balance. This also applies to mortgages and car loans. If possible, send extra money each month to pay the principal towards your mortgage loan. By paying one additional payment each year, you can eliminate seven years of interest from your loan. By paying an additional $50 or $100 to your car loan every month you can pay your car loan off before the scheduled end of loan date. By paying the mortgage loan or car loan by the scheduled end of loan date you end up paying two or three times what you originally borrowed on the loan. Below is Mary's budget and her list of debts.

Type of Bill	Monthly Payment	Priority of Bills (to Pay Off)	Balance Due
Visa	$ 30	3	$ 1,000
Student Loan	$ 70	4	$ 3,500
Macy's	$ 30	2	$ 1,200
MasterCard	$ 35	1	$ 370 (was 500)
Car Payment	$350	5	$12,000
Misc. Expenses	$200	———	———
Savings	$ 86	———	———
Totals	$801	———	$18,070

Table 2 – Mary's Budget to Pay off her Debts

In four months, Mary will have saved $344 (86 * 4) and paid her MasterCard bill ($100 * 4). The fifth month Mary can start sending $195 ($130 + $35 + $30 [$130 payment sent to her MasterCard bill + minimum payment on her MasterCard and Macy's bills]) a month to her Macy's bill and continue to send the minimum payments for all of her other bills. In five months Mary paid $315 (30 * 4 + $195 = $315) to her Macy's bill, she now owes $885. Mary will continue paying on her Macy's bill until it is paid and repeat the same process to pay off her Visa bill.

In one year Mary will have paid off her MasterCard and Macy's bills, increased her monthly payment on her Visa bill and will have paid: $690 ($195 + $195 + 30 * 10) on her Visa, $840 ($70 * 12) on her student loan and $4200 ($350 * 12) on her car.
Mary's total debt now is $10,770 ($18,070 − $4,200 [car] − $840 [student loan] − $690 [Visa] − $1,200 [Macy's] − $500 [MasterCard] = $10,770) and Mary has saved $1,032 (86 * 12).

Once your debts are paid then you can modify your budget to achieve other financial goals such as: purchase a home if you don't already have one, open an Individual Retirement Account (IRA), save money in a 401(k), open a CD, money market account or purchase rental property.

If you owed money to a taxing authority or had a lien on your property you can repair the damage to your credit report. Pay these debts as soon as possible and try to negotiate with the taxing authority for the amount owed and to remove the lien. If you owe back taxes you may not be able to negotiate the amount owed but you may be able to set up a payment plan. You can request an offer in compromise with the taxing authority which removes the lien from your property and begins reporting to the credit bureau agency that the lien has been removed. Consult a lawyer or Certified Public Accountant (CPA) familiar with your local and state laws and tax codes to advise you on how to best negotiate.

If you feel you have no money to begin paying off your debts, sell some assets such as jewelry, a second car and clothing. Find creative ways to come up with the money to pay off your debt. **Here are twelve additional ways to get money to pay off your debts:**

— Shop during sales for things you need (but don't use a sale as an excuse to buy things you don't need).

— Cancel your cable, pager, cellular phone and/or internet services. You can get a free internet mail account, such as hotmail or gmail, and check your messages at the local library.

— Buy store brands instead of name brands (i.e. grocery store, etc.).

— Join a wholesale club (i.e. Sam's, Costco).

— Catch public transportation to work or ride your bike.

— Cancel your long distance service on your home telephone.

— Turn off any unused utilities (electricity, turn heat or a/c down while you are at work or not in that room).

— Reduce the amount of money spent on gifts.

— Send e–cards (electronic cards using www.hallmark.com, etc.) instead of mailing cards to family and friends.

— Hold a yard sale to sell unused items.

— Use your tax refund.

— Get a second job.

Once you develop your budget remember to include these items in your budget. If you cannot set aside money for these items, you may need to include them in your future financial plans:

— You can begin the first step to creating a budget by opening a savings account and checking account.

— Open a retirement account.

— Invest your money.

— Call your local bank and inquire about opening a money market account.

— Talk to a financial advisor to discuss the various options available to you and how to set your immediate financial goals, as well as those for the future.

Remember to employ some of the practical and easy techniques I used to reduce expenses: pack your lunch, eat breakfast at home, carpool, take public transportation to work, rent movies instead of going to the movies and avoid paying just the minimum monthly payment on your credit cards.

This chapter helped you develop a spending plan (budget) to begin paying off your debts. Once you have determined what your expenses are, what is owed and how much money you have to work with, you can begin to set up a reasonable spending plan to pay off your debts. Some people may take drastic measures to pay off their debts quicker; some may take small steps which will take longer to pay off your debts. I took drastic measures because I felt overwhelmed.

A lot of tips were provided in this section. Don't worry if you don't use all of them. Identify what your top goals are and work towards those. Then come back to the list of tips and work towards accomplishing additional goals and keep doing that until you reach all of your goals.

Determine where you see yourself in the next year or two and take steps to get there. Don't be discouraged if you don't reach your goal in that year or two because you have taken steps to get there and in that year or two you will be in less debt than you are now.

Remember to encourage yourself and believe that you can do it (even if you have to say to yourself in the mirror every day, "I will be debt free, I will be debt free, this is only a temporary setback, I will overcome this!"). The next chapter will discuss how to get back on track after filing for bankruptcy.

Chapter 3 – Get Back on Track after a Bankruptcy

This chapter explains how to repair your credit even if you have filed for bankruptcy or have been reported to collection agencies, or have a lien, judgment or repossession. Bankruptcy is a process where a federal bankruptcy court allows you, as a consumer, to discharge all, or a portion of, your debt. A major benefit of bankruptcy is that as soon as you file your petition with the court asking to be declared bankrupt, all of your creditors identified in the bankruptcy are prevented from making attempts to collect money owed on your debts. A major disadvantage of bankruptcy is that it remains on your credit report for seven to ten years depending on the type of bankruptcy filed so use bankruptcy as an absolute last resort.

A trustee is appointed to handle each bankruptcy case. The trustee divides your assets among your creditors. Some of your assets are not considered such as a wedding ring, clothing, food, books, furniture, etc. The law varies from state to state concerning what assets are considered. To file for personal bankruptcy you must reside in a state for 90 days prior to filing and have a total unsecured debt less than $290,525 or secured debt less than $871,550. You can hire an attorney to assist you in filing for bankruptcy and pay attorney fees and a filing fee with the court. If you do not hire an attorney, go to the library or do research online to find out all the requirements and forms available to file for bankruptcy. However, before filing for bankruptcy be sure that there is no other way to get out of debt as your income and totals debts are evaluated before being considered for bankruptcy. You may also be required to attend budgeting or money management courses.

Unfortunately it is harder than ever to file for bankruptcy. A new bankruptcy law enacted in October 2005 states that debtors (consumers) who earn less than the median income in their state about 80 percent of those who file for bankruptcy still would be entitled to file under Chapter 7. But those who earn more than that and who have the ability to repay at least $6,000 over five years would have to file under Chapter 13, which requires a repayment plan. If you are considering filing for bankruptcy, read the first seven chapters of this book to see if you can avoid it.

There are two kinds of personal bankruptcy, Chapter 7 and Chapter 13. You may be encouraged to file Chapter 13 instead of Chapter 7 bankruptcy. Chapter 7 bankruptcy, also called liquidation, uses a trustee who determines the assets you can keep. All other assets are turned over to the trustee who may sell them at a public auction and divide the proceeds among your creditors. **You will still be responsible for some debts such as:**

- Students loans
- Taxes or Tax Liens
- Alimony
- Child support

Chapter 13 bankruptcy is also called reorganization, and allows an individual to keep all of their property while repaying their bills. The court provides full legal protection from your creditors and you must be employed and earn enough income to pay reduced living expenses and repay your debts over a period of time. You must submit a budget to the court which is reviewed and turned into a monthly payment plan. Payments are made directly to the court, which pays your creditors. If you are ever late with payments your case will be dismissed.

If you are considering filling for Chapter 13 bankruptcy, consider that a better option may be to develop payment plans and negotiate repayment of your debts yourself. Chapter 7 bankruptcy appears on your credit report for up to ten years. Chapter 13 appears on your credit report for up to seven years.

Filing for bankruptcy may tempt you when your money problems overwhelm you. Don't let emotions rule your actions. Try to find other ways to pay off your debts. If you have to file for bankruptcy, be careful about establishing your credit. Once you have obtained a copy of your credit report from all three credit reporting agencies, review your reports to make sure that the bankruptcy account(s) are listed as discharged.

Filing for bankruptcy affects your credit when applying for a job, for credit, a loan or renting an apartment. The IRS gets a report of all bankruptcy settlements and considers as income any debt from which you are released (no longer have to pay). The IRS will tax you on that amount. Contact your local tax office for more information. Bankruptcy fees are also required when applying for bankruptcy so if you are living paycheck to paycheck you may not be able to afford to file for bankruptcy. If you file bankruptcy through a lawyer, the lawyer also charges fees to file the bankruptcy which could put you further in debt.

After filing for bankruptcy, wait at **least** two years before applying for a mortgage or car loan to get the best interest rate you can. If not, you may risk the chance of getting a higher interest rate and get further in debt. Also, mortgage lenders will be more willing to approve you for a loan provided that you have not had any delinquencies in the past two years. You may get a higher interest rate but you can always refinance within 6 months to get a lower interest rate. It may be easier for you to purchase a Housing and Urban Development (HUD) home by financing with a FHA loan. The requirements are not as strict as those for conventional loans. You should also consider rent–to–own homes and foreclosures.

If you have an account that is in collection, this is due to a bill not being paid on time or a bill that has not been paid, the creditor can write the account off as a bad debt and send it to a collection agency. This type of account is displayed on your credit report as chargeoff" or "collection". The creditor does not have to wait a specified period of time before sending the account to a collection agency, but most wait three or four months before doing so.

Sometimes if a creditor is unable to receive payment they will close the account preventing the customer from using the account. This type of account is displayed on your credit report as "account closed by credit grantor".

If you have missed some payments to a creditor you can contact the creditor before the account is sent to a collection agency to arrange a payment plan. In some cases, for an account that has been "charged off," you can still negotiate a settlement payment with the creditor if you are unable to pay the full amount.

Because of my bad credit most of my accounts were sent to collection agencies, so I set up payment plans with each collection agency and began making payments. Many collection agencies are willing to work with you; you just have to take the first step to contact them. If you have an account that has been reported to a collection agency, it is not the end of the world. However, if you are unable to pay the collection agency, notify them immediately and try to set up a payment plan that enables you to pay the debt owed in a realistic time frame. If you can pay a small amount on the account every month, do so and keep records of all payments made.

Some creditors will negotiate with you and reduce the amount owed and ask for a lump sum amount to settle the account in exchange for paying the debt quickly, although it is best to pay the full amount. Be sure not to make promises to a creditor or collection agency that you will not be able to keep. If your financial situation changes in any way and you are not able to continue the payments, notify the collection agency immediately and try to negotiate other arrangements. Remember to write down each person's name that you speak with, date/time and what was said or write a letter to confirm agreements made or conversations held concerning your account.

You can obtain a secured credit card until your debts are paid. A secured credit card is when you put a deposit in the bank and obtain a credit line equal to one and a half times the amount of your deposit. The deposit acts as collateral, which the bank can draw from if you do not pay on time. This secures the card. Often times you have to meet certain requirements for a secured card, such as length of time at your current residence and salary.

Make sure the creditor reports your payments to the credit reporting agencies, has a grace period and does not report your credit card as a secured card. You can contact the creditor and ask them about the policy for secured cards before obtaining an account. You can also obtain a signature loan at a bank or credit union where you have a savings account. Only borrow a small amount of money, using the savings account as collateral.

You can also request that delinquent accounts be removed before 7 years. There is no law that states that delinquent accounts have to remain on your credit report for seven years but the Federal Credit Reporting Act (FCRA) law does state that negative information can remain on your credit report for **up to** 7 years.

If you live in a fairly safe community and can catch public transportation to work, do so. If you absolutely need a car to get around, consider buying a used car, a car from a friend or neighbor, or apply for a car loan for no more than three or four years. If you get a loan for more than three years, the car might soon be worth much less than the amount owed on it. If it stops working, you'll need to pay off the loan – far more than what you can get for it. If you need to sell it try to sell it for what is owed on the loan or near what is owed. Check the blue book value to make sure your selling price is not too high. If you don't get any offers you might have to lower your selling price.

Before applying for a car loan make sure the lender is a reputable lender. Be wary of the "bad credit – no problem" lenders. You may be able to buy a car, but you may also get a bad deal or strict terms in the contract. Have someone review the contract before you sign it and ask questions about any information that you do not understand and any fees that may seem confusing.

If you have recently obtained more than one new credit card cut up all but one with the lowest limit. If you have more than three credit cards, cut up all unnecessary credit cards such as department store and gas cards. Close the accounts and cancel the credit cards and keep open the remaining credit cards with the longest good credit history (no late payments). Remember when repairing your credit; don't open any new accounts because this will decrease your credit score.

If you have delinquent credit that includes a tax debt or tax lien, try to pay this debt in full as soon as possible. If you owe money to the IRS or a state income taxing authority, you can negotiate to pay less than the full amount owed and remove the lien from your property. Obtain a letter from the IRS or state taxing authority indicating the lien was removed. Once you receive the letter, write the credit reporting agencies to inform them that the lien has been removed.

You must complete a form 656 Offer in Compromise to negotiate with the IRS. This form can be found by going to the IRS website at ww.irs.gov or contact your local IRS office and request that a form be mailed to you. Keep in mind the form has a filing fee. You can negotiate the amount owed if: the amount owed is not part of a lawsuit, there is doubt that you owe the IRS, and if the IRS will be able to collect the full amount owed including penalties and interest.

You must prove to the IRS that you do not owe the amount in question or that the amount owed is incorrect by providing copies of receipts, cancelled checks, tax forms, or signed correspondence. You should verify your actions with a lawyer or CPA who is familiar with the IRS local or state tax codes.

If you owe back taxes the taxing authority may not accept less than what you owe but you can negotiate a payment plan that can eliminate debt over time by making installment payments. Once the taxing authority agrees to remove the lien you must begin making installment payments or pay off a certain amount owed. Call the appropriate taxing authority if you wish to set up a payment plan. If you are unable to talk to someone who is willing to work with you, ask to speak to someone else or ask to speak to a supervisor.

Make sure you file taxes every year and pay any taxes owed every year or you may have your wages garnished or end up in jail. Even a few celebrities, who shall remain nameless, have headed to the slammer for tax evasion. If you owe the IRS taxes then a lien can be placed against you (this depends on the amount owed and how long you have owed that amount). A lien is a court order that gives a creditor an interest in a piece of real property or personal property that you own (home, condominium, boat, or other personal property). If you ever sell the property, the creditor must be paid from the money made from the sale.

Once a lien is placed against your property you must pay the lien or try to negotiate a settlement with the creditor for removing it. Once you have paid a federal tax lien, request a Certificate of Release of Federal Tax Lien from the IRS indicating that the lien is paid in full. Then have the credit reporting agencies contact the IRS to verify the release of the lien. This can be done by writing a letter to the credit reporting agencies and providing information on how to contact the IRS (specifically the person you talked to and a contact number) along with a copy of the Certificate of Release of Federal Tax Lien form that was sent to the IRS. For a lien with a creditor you should receive a copy of the Claim of Lien or some similar form. Once the lien is paid request a copy of the Release of Lien form indicating that the lien is paid, verify the release of the lien, and send a copy to the three credit reporting agencies.

If you had a judgment placed against you this is the last resort for a company to collect a debt. The debt owed was transferred to a collection agency that made several attempts to collect the money owed. Since they did not receive a response from you they referred the account to the courts and filed a judgment against you. In order to obtain a judgment, the creditor must sue in the state where the consumer resides.

For signed contracts, creditors can seek a judgment in the state where the contract was signed. The judgment is reported on your credit report and remains there. It gives a creditor the right to collect the money owed by garnishing your wages or paycheck, seizing your personal property or real estate or seizing your assets or bank accounts. You can still try to negotiate with the creditor to pay the full amount or for a settlement (amount you suggest instead of paying the full amount owed). You should have received a document from the court stating the date of the judgment and the amount of the judgment. Make sure you have a legal document identifying the terms of the settlement before sending in the money. Also before sending any money for the settlement request a letter in writing from the creditor that the judgment will be removed from your credit report and reported to the three credit reporting agencies once the full amount or settlement amount is received.

Once you receive that letter then send your payment along with the signed settlement agreement. Make sure that you receive proof of payment for the judgment and keep these documents for future reference. Once the debt is paid the court records the judgment has been satisfied and indicates this on your credit report.

Then you must file a judgment discharge with the court to indicate that you paid the amount owed. You should receive one but, if not, request one. You may have to insist that the creditor file this document with the court. Make sure you get a copy of all of the documentation relating to the judgment and when the judgment is satisfied. Check you credit report to make sure the judgment states that it has been satisfied. If it is not reflected on your credit report contact the court and the creditor to let them know and get a response in writing when your credit report has been updated.

If you feel that a judgment was not legally served or was not served properly you can: file a pre–trial request asking that the case be dismissed because the summons or complaint was not legally served; or by arguing at the trial that the complaint was not legally served. The trial will be postponed or the plaintiff (company who filed the judgment against you) will have to re–serve a new complaint.

In some cases, a consumer is considered "judgment proof" because they have no assets or very little income. If you are "judgment proof" then the creditor has nothing to take and there is no need to try and negotiate a settlement unless you are able to borrow the money from a friend or relative. Lawsuits or judgments can appear on your credit report for up to seven years or the time period stated in the statute of limitations, whichever is longer. Refer to Appendix E for more information.

If a creditor is unable to receive payment from you for a debt in some cases they can garnish your wages to collect the debt. This is arranged through your employer and the money is taken from your paycheck until the debt is paid. This rarely happens but if it does there is not much you can do. However, when you are notified from your employer that this will occur you can still contact the creditor and try to setup a settlement for the debt owed. This will probably only work if you have at least 50% of the amount owed because the creditor wants their money.

If you are unable to negotiate with the creditor then you will have to get prepared for the garnishment of your wages. If possible, while your wages are being garnished try getting a part–time job or cut down on your expenses to offload the money coming out of your paycheck.

If your wages are garnished your employer will send you a letter listing the amount that will be garnished and when the garnishment will begin. Make sure you request a copy of the Request for Garnishment Wages form from the court if you do not receive one.

If your bank account is seized as a result of garnishment your account(s) will remain frozen until all the funds owed have been paid. You should immediately notify your creditors for any checks written, try to borrow money to pay the checks written or stop payment on the checks to prevent the checks from bouncing and making your credit even worse. If you have a joint bank account with someone other than your spouse and that person's name was not on the judgment account that bank account cannot be seized.

If you have a joint account and the primary owner's name of the account did not appear on the judgment account they are not responsible for that account and therefore cannot have their bank account seized. You cannot garnish funds from a jointly held account unless your judgment was against both owners. When you are notified that your bank account will be seized ask the creditor for a copy of the Request for Garnishment of Property other than Wages form. If you agree to the garnishment a writ and a Garnishee Confession of Assets of Property other than Wages form will be submitted to your bank.

The bank has 30 days from the date of the receipt to file with the court and a copy should be mailed to you. Seizing personal property or real estate is the hardest type of judgment to obtain and is the most expensive due to the many forms and court fees. It is rare that personal property is seized to pay a debt.

If you fail to pay your monthly car payment your car can be repossessed by the finance company. Repossession usually occurs after 90 days of failing to make a payment. Your car will be towed and this will be reported on your credit report. To prevent your car from being repossessed you can work out a settlement plan to pay back the money owed and become current on your account. Make sure you get the settlement agreement in writing and request that once the account is current the delinquent account is removed from your credit report.

Here are four tips to remember when you consider filing for bankruptcy:

- Use bankruptcy as an absolute last resort.
- To file for bankruptcy you must reside in a state for 90 days prior to filing.
- A new bankruptcy law enacted in October 2005 states that consumers who earn less than the median income in their state about 80 percent of those who file for bankruptcy still would be entitled to file under Chapter 7. But those who earn more than that and who have the ability to repay at least $6,000 over five years would have to file under Chapter 13, which requires a repayment plan.
- Applying for bankruptcy affects your credit when applying for a job, credit, a loan or to rent an apartment.

Here are two tips if you have filed for bankruptcy:
- Wait at **least** two years before applying for a mortgage, car loan, or credit card to get the best interest rate you possibly can. If not, you may risk the chance of getting a higher interest rate and sink deeper into debt.
- Be wary of the "bad credit – no problem" lenders. You may be able to buy a car, but you may also get a bad deal or strict terms in the contract such as making a larger down payment.

Here are five tips if you have a debt that is in collection, a judgment, lien, garnishment or repossession:

- Contact the creditor immediately to try to setup a settlement or payment plan.
- Keep records of all correspondence sent to and received from the creditor.
- Get a part–time job and reduce expenses to help with paying the debt.
- Don't file for bankruptcy to avoid paying the debt.
- Once the debt is paid ensure it is reported correctly on your credit report.

This chapter explored bankruptcy, collections, judgments, garnishments, liens, and repossessions. Think long and hard before filing for bankruptcy. The ultimate goal is to get out of debt and have good credit. Filing for bankruptcy will only prolong the length of time you have bad credit. If you follow the steps in the first three chapters you will be able to get out of debt without filing for bankruptcy, having your account(s) go to a collection agency, having your wages garnished, or a lien or judgment filed against you. The next chapter will discuss how to repair your credit if you are a widow or divorcee. Good luck!

Chapter 4 – Women and Their Credit

This chapter discusses how to deal with credit issues if you are a widow, divorcee or common law spouse. Your spouse is not legally responsible for any debt incurred before you were married. However, when most couples get married they willingly take on each other's debts. Note: please do not use this statement as a reason to start an argument with your spouse about his or her debts prior to you getting married. If you do not wish to pay your future spouses debt then make sure that both of you have setup a payment plan to become debt free or almost debt free before getting married, discuss all of your debts and expenses before getting married. If you are not sure where to start you can consult with a credit expert like me at hfreeman@hefreemanenterprises.com.

If you have a joint account with a spouse you are responsible for that debt. If you become a widow or widower and you have a joint account with a spouse that has passed away you are still held responsible for those debts. If your spouse that has passed away had any individual accounts such as credit cards, loans, etc. (with their name only on the accounts) you are not held responsible. You can write a letter to each creditor and notify them that your spouse has passed. The creditor may state that you are held responsible and have to pay those debts but legally you do not have to pay them.

However, if your spouse that has passed away had assets such as a car, house, stocks, bonds, bank accounts, etc. (individual or joint), his or her creditors can be subject to probate (they can file charges against his or her estate) and his or her assets can be used to pay his or her creditors. You must contact a lawyer in your state to find out the laws for probate estates (this means the living spouse could be held liable for the former spouse's debt based on certain state laws).

If the deceased spouse's estate distributes estate property to its beneficiaries before all debts of the deceased person have been paid, the creditor can recover all or part of the debt out of the property distributed to the beneficiary. The creditor cannot get money for the debt from the beneficiary's other property, only the property received from the estate can be accessed by creditors.

If you are legally separated contact a lawyer in your state to find out state laws regarding debt, joint accounts and marital property rights. During separation get a copy of your credit report to verify its accuracy which will enable you to address any issues with your spouse before the divorce is finalized. If your spouse agrees to pay some of the debt during separation, write letters to all the creditors for your joint accounts and indicate that your spouse will pay those debts and if payment is not received to contact your spouse only not you for payment. Once the divorce is final neither spouse is responsible for the other's debt. Sometimes a creditor will not honor your request so to further ensure that you are not held responsible contact the creditors to close all joint accounts and cancel the credit cards.

If you are in the process of going through a divorce ask your lawyer to include all joint accounts in the divorce settlement. You have several options, you can request in the divorce decree that your spouse pay 50% of the debts owed and you pay the other 50%; or if you cannot afford to pay all or some of the debt on the joint accounts ask your spouse if he or she can pay more than 50% of the debts. If you feel your spouse will not keep the agreement you can ask the judge to request that the spouse send payments to the court who will then send payments to the creditor. If your spouse falls behind in payments and the late payments are reported on your credit report you can ask that the agreement is null and void and have your spouse pay all of the debt for the joint accounts. The judge may not grant this but it is worth a try. If there are any accounts that are in your spouses' name only and you can prove that you did not make any charges you can ask the judge to hold your spouse responsible to pay those debts. If you cannot prove that you did not make any charges on those accounts it may be harder to get the judge to hold your spouse responsible for those debts.

While going through your divorce you should close all joint accounts and cancel the credit cards where your former spouse was an authorized user. If your spouse had an individual account but added you as an "authorized user" that could make charges on the account you will not be legally held responsible for any debt owed. You should also close these accounts because they will be reported on your credit report and your former spouse's credit report.

If you are unable to close the account ask that your name be removed as an authorized user and get it in writing from the creditor. Notify the creditors that any debt incurred after the date of the letter you will not be held liable. Send the letter by certified mail as proof of receipt. You could also write a letter to the creditor to request a conversion of the joint accounts to individual accounts. It is up to the creditor to decide if an account will be converted based on a change in marital status. The creditor may request that you re–apply for the individual account if you relied on your ex–husband's income to obtain the credit. Based on the Equal Credit Opportunity Act which gives women ways to build their own credit, a creditor should allow you to open an individual credit account in your name. The creditor must respond within 30 days of receiving your application. Also, ask the creditor to consider the credit history of your former spouse's (if it is good) and the credit history reported in your name if you have any.

Having individual credit can be very helpful if your former spouse had bad credit and will enable you to keep your good credit after the divorce. If you are not able to convert the joint accounts then close them immediately and pay the balance owed as soon as possible.

Unfortunately a closed account can be re–opened at any time so your former spouse could re–open the account and continue making purchases which is why you must also ask that the credit card be cancelled so your credit will not be affected.

A creditor cannot make you reapply for credit because you were married, become a widow or divorced. They also can't close your account or change the terms of your account because you become married, a widow or divorced. If this happens to you tell the creditor that they are violating federal law and file a complaint against them.

If your former spouses falls behind in payments you could still be held liable for the debts even though you have a divorcee decree indicating your former spouse will pay the debts because the creditor is not bound by the terms of the divorce decree. You should also consider selling or refinancing in one spouse's name loans that are held jointly such as a car loan or mortgage loan.

After your divorce immediately contact all of your creditors and notify them in writing that you just went through a divorce. Also notify them of any joint accounts that you will have to pay. If you are not able to pay the debts owed let your creditors know and setup a payment plan so your credit is not affected by the divorce. If you are unable to pay the debts or setup a payment plan you may have to get a part–time job.

If you live in a community property (common law) state you and your spouse are responsible for debts incurred together. The following states recognize common law marriage: Arizona, California, Idaho, Louisiana, Nevada, New Mexico, Texas, Washington, Wisconsin, Puerto Rico, and Washington, DC. Individual debts of one spouse may appear on the credit report of the other spouse. In these states a creditor has the right to ask a woman about her marital status and request information about her husband if her husband will be held responsible for the debt or if the woman is relying on her husband's income to help make the payments. If a woman uses property that is jointly owned by her and her husband as collateral, a creditor may require that her husband cosign the loan even if the woman will be solely responsible for repayment. Also, contact your state government to find out about common law and marital property rights in your state.

Information provided in this chapter is general information that will point you in the right direction. This chapter provided information regarding debt for divorcees, widows, widowers and common law spouses. Please note I am not a lawyer or expert on financial matters regarding widows, widowers, divorcees and common law marriage, so please contact your local or state government for laws concerning these matters. Whatever your situation if you follow the steps outlined in chapters one through seven you will be well on your way to achieving "A" credit. The next chapter will discuss how to repair your credit.

Chapter 5 – How to Repair Your Credit

This chapter explains how to repair your credit no matter what your credit score or financial situation. Since your credit is so important and affects so many aspects of your life you should protect it as you would protect yourself and your life. If, for some reason, you fall behind in your credit card payments or loan payments due to unemployment, health conditions, financial burdens, etc., notify your creditor(s) immediately and set up a payment plan. Some creditors participate in a debt repayment program. Sometimes there is a fee for the debt repayment program, usually a small percentage of what is owed to the creditors. Some credit card companies have insurance that will automatically make payments on your account(s) until you are able to regain employment. This helps prevent negative marks on your credit report. You will have to weigh the costs of these programs with what you can afford and the specific rules that apply when signing up for these programs.

Because I was willing to set up payment plans with my creditors, they were willing to work with me to restore my credit and remove the delinquencies on my credit report. I was honest with each one and stated that I had lost my job, which is why I fell behind in payments. It took trial and error when I began writing letters to each of my creditors to set up payment plans and restore my credit. Finally, I was able to develop good letters and repair each of my credit problems which I have used with my clients. Many of the creditors provided me with valuable information for the future. For example: "If you ever fall behind in your payments again, notify us immediately," as well as other information which I am passing on to you through this book. And, yes, I promise to include sample letters which took me so long to perfect!

You have created a budget for yourself and have begun paying down some of your debt. Now it is time to negotiate and begin repairing your credit. One important tool in repairing your credit is to educate yourself, do research and find out what your rights are as a consumer. Find out about a creditor's policies and about the credit reporting agencies' polices. Attend seminars, subscribe to newsletters, go to the library or do research about credit and credit repair.

While you are in the process of repairing your credit, if a creditor continues to call you and is harassing you, inform them of your particular situation, get the person's name, date and time they called and tell them when you will be able to make a payment. If they continue to call you after that, inform them that you will report them to the Federal Trade Commission (FTC) Consumer Response Center for harassment, and that you can sue them in court for violation of the Federal Credit Reporting Act (FCRA).

Another way to prevent creditors from calling you is by using a service that Verizon has called "call intercept." This forces a person to identify themselves if their telephone number appears as "out of area", "unavailable", "anonymous", or "private" on your caller id. If the person refuses to identify himself or herself, the call will not go through. You can also register your phone number with the FTC by going to www.donotcall.gov and adding your number to the "do not call list" or by calling 888–382–1222, or TDD (for the hearing impaired) 866–290–4236.

If you are late in paying a monthly debt, you can ask the creditor not to report the information to a collection agency. Unfortunately, most of us do not know when our account will be reported. You can negotiate with the creditor and get the monthly payment reduced without being penalized or you can negotiate a settlement payment. Notify the creditor in writing (or collection agency if it has already been reported to a collection agency) that you will send the settlement amount in exchange that the delinquent account is removed from your credit report and ask them to notify you when the account is removed from your credit report. Once you receive a response from the creditor that they agree to this then send in your settlement payment via certified mail.

Get a copy of your credit report at least once a year from the three major credit reporting agencies, Equifax, Experian and TransUnion, especially when making large purchases such as a car, home, etc. Your credit score is not affected when you obtain your credit report. It is only affected when you apply for a credit card or line of credit such as a car, home, or other loan. You can go to www.myfico.com and get a combined credit report from all three credit reporting agencies and a copy of your credit score for a fee. You can now get a free copy of your credit report at www.annualcreditreport.com or by calling 877–322–8228 or TDD (for the hearing impaired) 877–730–4104, which has been validated by the three major credit reporting bureau agencies. You can also get a copy of your credit score on this website for a nominal fee.

There are some restrictions with getting the credit report, but to start repairing your credit they are small potatoes. Some states allow you to obtain one free credit report a year. Be wary of websites that state they will give you a free copy of your credit report. You can not verify how your personal information is stored and who will have access to it and if that information is protected or forwarded to other companies for various reasons. You may have to pay a fee depending on what state you live in if you have already obtained a credit report in less than 12 months. Find out the laws for your particular state for obtaining a credit report. Refer to Appendix F for more information. You can find this information on the internet, the library or by calling one of the three credit reporting agencies who may be able to tell you the law in your particular state. You can also read the FCRA to obtain information about your credit and the laws concerning creditors and your rights, at www.ftc.gov and view the text of the FCRA 15 U.S.C. 1681–1681u.

The names and addresses of the three most popular credit reporting agencies are listed. It is best to use these to repair your credit instead of using a third party credit report from your mortgage company, loan officer or other party trying to offer you credit or a loan since the majority of businesses that report your credit history use these credit reporting agencies. It is better to update your information with the source or originator of the information. The information reported to other credit reporting agencies are less popular and it is harder to correct information from those than the three major credit reporting agencies. The fact is many of the other credit reporting agencies get their information from the three major credit reporting agencies.

Equifax Credit Information Services
P.O. Box 740256
Atlanta, GA 30374
800–685–1111
866–478–0030 (TDD)
www.equifax.com

Experian
NCAC
P.O. Box 9595
Allen, TX 75013–9595
888–397–3742 (and TDD)
www.experian.com

TransUnion
P.O. Box 1000
Chester, PA 19022–1000
800–916–8800
877–553–7803 (TDD)
www.tuc.com

If you have bounced checks, you can contact the main check verification registries, Chexsystems or Telecheck to get a free copy of your check report every year. Bounced checks remain on your credit report for five years.

Chex Systems, Inc.
Attn: Consumer Relations
7805 Hudson Road, Suite 100
Woodbury, MN 55125
800–428–9623
www.consumerdebit.com

TeleCheck Services, Inc.
5251 Westheimer
Houston, Texas 77056
800–TELECHECK
www.telecheck.com

You can request a copy of your credit report by completing an online request, calling or sending a letter requesting your credit report. **The quickest way to obtain your credit report is by ordering it online by going to www.annualcreditreport.com.**

The following is a sample letter that can be sent to request a copy of your credit report.

Equifax
P.O. Box 740256
Atlanta, GA 30374
Current Date

To Whom It May Concern:

I am writing to request a copy of my most recent credit report. I have enclosed a check in the amount of $10 (or whatever the fee is in your state and only applies if you have received a copy of your credit report in less than a 12 month time period). My information is listed below. Thank you.

Susie Joan Smith (Full Name including suffixes, Jr., etc.)
Current Address
Social Security Number

Sincerely,

Your Name
Street Address
City, State, ZipCode

Verify all the information that appears on your credit report is correct. If it is not, the credit reporting agency usually sends an investigation form along with a copy of your report, if not you can request one be mailed to you. Complete the form and provide as much detail as possible about the errors. Also provide any documentation to support your reason for the investigation and attach a letter explaining the reason you wish to have the information investigated. Be sure to highlight or identify the incorrect information and any updates that need to be made. Include your name, social security number, and current and previous address (if you have moved within the last 5 years). You can also request that the updated information be sent to certain creditors and employers and request written confirmation that the updated information was sent.

Keep a copy of the information sent to the credit reporting agency. The information must be removed or corrected within 30 days of the receipt of your investigation form by the credit reporting agency if the information on the credit report is inaccurate or can no longer be verified. This can be found in section 611 of the FCRA. It is always best to request an investigation through the mail because you will have a written record and copies of your supporting documentation.

Once the investigation is complete you will be notified by mail by the credit reporting agency. The credit reporting agency may send you a full copy of your credit report or may just send the corrections. **Once you obtain a copy of your credit report, verify that the information updated is correct. Wait two to three months and request another copy of your credit report to ensure that the incorrect information was updated and no other errors appear on your credit report.** If you do not receive an updated credit report or a response to your investigation within 30 days from the day the credit reporting agency receives your request – usually 5 to 7 days from when you mailed the request, contact the credit reporting agency and request a status of the investigation.

If inaccurate information reappears on your credit report, ensure that the credit reporting agency has provided you with a reason why the information was put back on your credit report. If you are unable to get the incorrect information removed, try to find additional documentation to support your claim, contact the company that provided the incorrect information and request that the information be corrected and provided to all three credit reporting agencies, or you can call your local state attorney general's office of consumer affairs and explain your situation to get guidance on what your options are. You can contact the Federal Trade Commission (FTC) if you have a problem with a credit reporting agency. You can also contact your local Better Business Bureau (BBB) to find out what your legal rights.

Be sure to keep copies of all correspondence you send to the credit reporting agency regarding your credit report and any correspondence that is sent to you from the credit reporting agency. You may need this information in the future. Also keep any receipts for accounts for which you have made payments on or paid in full. Keep receipts for accounts paid in full for at least one year. For accounts that were delinquent and have been paid in full, request a letter from the creditor stating that the account was paid in full to ensure that if the account is not updated, removed or reappears on your credit report, you have proof from the creditor that it was paid in full.

Negative information on your credit report can remain for up to seven years. Bankruptcies and collections can remain on your credit report for up to ten years. Non–negative information can remain on your credit report for up to ten years. Don't worry about removing non–negative information from your credit report because this is used to calculate your credit score and it helps when repairing your credit. Obtain a copy of your credit report once the specific time period for removal of your delinquent accounts has arrived. If these items have not been removed from your credit report, write the credit reporting agency to have them removed. A few sample letters to help you restore your credit appear in the following pages.

This letter is to request that an inquiry that is 2 old be removed from the credit report.

Equifax
P.O. Box 740256
Atlanta, GA 30374
Current Date

To Whom It May Concern:

I received a copy of my credit report and am writing this letter to request that the inquiry on my credit report for Bank of America be removed since this inquiry is two years old as of December 13, 2005. Please notify me in writing when this request is processed. Thank you.

Sincerely,

Your Name
Street Address
City, State, ZipCode
SSN

This letter is to request a delinquent account be removed from your credit report.

Company ABC
P. O. Box 123
City, State, Zip Code
Current Date

To Whom It May Concern:

I am in the process or buying a home (buying a car, etc.) and am requesting that my Visa account# 123456789 be removed from my credit report since this account was opened on 1/1/85, closed on 4/12/99 and is now paid in full. I was not able to pay this account due to other financial obligations (or whatever your situation). Since that time I have paid all my debts on time. Please report this information Equifax, Experian, and TransUnion. Please notify me in writing when this request has been processed. Thank you.

Sincerely,

Your Name
Street Address
City, State, ZipCode

This letter is to set up a payment plan for a delinquent account.

Company ABC
P. O. Box 123
City, State, Zip Code
Current Date

To Whom It May Concern:

I would like to set up a payment plan for my Macy's account#
1234567890. Due to loss of employment (or whatever the reason) I
fell behind on my payments but am now able to make payments. I
am able to pay $100 (or whatever amount you can pay) a month until
the debt is paid in full. Upon the bill being paid in full, please
update: my account status to "Paid in Full" and update my account
rating to "R1" on my credit report. Please report this information to
Experian, Equifax, and TransUnion. Please notify me in writing if
this payment plan agreement is accepted.

Sincerely,

Your Name
Street Address
City, State, ZipCode

This letter is to add a statement disputing inaccurate information on your credit report.

Equifax
P.O. Box 740256
Atlanta, GA 30374
Current Date

To Whom It May Concern:

The information reported on my credit report for Visa account#xxxxxxxxxxxxxxxx is incorrect. Please add the following statement to my credit report, "Customer disputes the status of this account. This account is not delinquent and no late payments have been made. Customer has tried to get the status of this account corrected but has been unable to do so" (you can add more details). Please send an updated credit report.

Sincerely,

Your Name
Street Address
City, State, ZipCode
SSN

You can use the sample letters as a guide. Rewrite the letters in your own words but remember to highlight the main points in the letter. **It is important to rewrite the letter in your own words because now many people are using credit counselors to assist them in repairing their credit.** If the credit reporting agencies see many of the same kinds of letters from various consumers they automatically assume that the letter is from a credit counseling agency and may not respond to the letter. **The key to writing letters to set up payment plans to pay your delinquent accounts is:**

- Be honest, humble and sincere.
- Identify any terms and negotiations you would like to make.
- Stick to the terms in your letter.
- Reassure the company that it will not happen again and that you appreciate them doing business with you.

If you are unable to remove negative information from your credit report you can write a 100 word statement to add to your credit file to dispute the negative information. When applying for new credit, inform the creditor that you have a 100 word statement in your file and that you would like the creditor to read it.

You can also try to locate new information relating to the dispute and send all previous and new information along with a letter explaining the error to the credit reporting agency. You can write the creditor a letter and ask that the problem be corrected on your credit file. Request that the correction be sent to you and all three credit reporting agencies. You can also contact your state's Attorney General's Office of Consumer Affairs to ask for help.

If you were declined credit for any reason, are unemployed, or on welfare, you can obtain a copy of your credit report for free. If you were declined credit due to an error on your credit report, complete an investigation form and send it to the credit reporting agency and notify the creditor that your credit report was incorrect and that you would like to apply for credit again. You may have to wait a certain period of time before you are eligible to apply for credit again depending on the creditor, usually three to six months. If you have been denied credit you can obtain a free copy of your credit report from the credit reporting agency that denied you credit.

However, you must request the credit report within sixty days of your denial and contact the company that denied you credit to get the name and address of the credit reporting agency that provided the negative information. If you have been or feel you have been the victim of credit fraud or identity theft, or if a collection agency notifies you that they reported or will report negative information about you to a credit reporting agency you can also receive a free copy of your credit report.

The balances displayed on your credit report may not reflect your most recent balance and could be one to two months behind your current account balance. Contact the credit reporting agencies to ensure that the correct information appears on your credit file with them.

If you have several credit card balances, leave your credit cards at home, and stay out of the malls and other stores to avoid shopping sprees. If you have more than five delinquent accounts that are still open, close two of them with the lowest credit limit and/or highest interest rates and cancel the credit cards. You can still continue to pay on an account even though it is closed; this will benefit you later when the date of last activity is reported for that account, and you wish to have the account removed. Cut up the credit cards for the accounts that you closed. **Here are nine common methods that you can use to pay off high interest debt:**

— If you have cash in the bank earning only a few percent, you are losing that interest rate because you are not making enough of a profit on your savings, so you can use it to pay down your debt. (If you have $4,000 saved don't take the entire $4,000 to pay down your debt, take half of that or 1/3 of that to pay off your debts and put the remaining amount in the bank or a money market account to earn a higher interest rate).

— If you have equity in your home, a home equity loan can be used to pay off your high interest credit cards. Sometimes the Annual

Percentage Rate (APR) on a home equity loan can be less than credit cards, and the interest on home equity loans may be tax deductible, which offsets the high APR on your credit card. Don't borrow more than 80% of the equity in your home. You can't write off the interest if you borrow more than what the home is worth. You may also be charged points at closing so be sure to account for those in your financial analysis.

— If you own stock that's performing badly and it would create a loss for you by selling it, and if you expect to have gains this year from your other stocks, one solution is to sell your bad stock at a loss to offset your taxable gains, then use the proceeds of the sale to pay off your credit card debt, which is losing you 18% APR. This just created 2 financial advantages for you.

— For a stock that is making money you could sell the stock at a profit, then use the profit to pay down your debt, which is losing you 18% APR. Many people only focus on their stock market gains but fail to realize that credit card debt at 18% erases those gains.

— If you have a retirement account through your job, some companies allow you to borrow against this account and pay yourself back with interest. This can be a good way to earn more interest on your retirement funds, but this is also risky. If you default on this loan, you lose your retirement money. You should seek the advice of a financial advisor before applying for this type of loan.

— Get a part–time job to earn extra income to pay your debts.
— Take training classes or get a college degree to gain extra skills to get a promotion.
— Use coupons and shop at wholesale stores like Costco or Sam's Club and use the money saved to pay down your debt.
— Reduce your expenses, cancel your cable service, cell phone service or get the cheapest plan available, pack your lunch, don't eat carry out food or go out to eat.

Don't use credit cards. Try to pay for purchases with cash or checks until your credit card balances are paid in full. Spread your holiday shopping and spending throughout the year to take advantage of sales and stick to a budget. Join a credit union. Some credit unions are more lenient when allowing members to apply for credit depending on their account history.

If you do use your credit card try to send in your monthly payment as soon as you receive the bill or soon after, or at least ten days before the due date, this gives the company plenty of time to process the payment before the due date. However, if you bill arrives just before the due date and your account is not charged finance or other charges before a certain date, the creditor must mail your bill at least 14 days before your payment is due. Otherwise you will have to pay the late charges because the creditor may state you are aware of when the bill is due and should have already sent your payment in (even though you did not receive the bill).

Some companies which shall remain nameless hold payments received until after the due date and process the payment which will be considered late. However, this is against the law and creditors must credit payments on the day they arrive provided the payment is sent to the correct mailing address. File a complaint against the company if you are a victim of this. To avoid this contact your local post office to find out how long it takes for mail from your area to arrive at the creditor's mailing address.

You can also call the creditor and ask how long it takes them to process out of state checks for payment. Once you gather this information then you can determine how soon you need to send in your payment to ensure that it is processed before the due date. Make sure you read the information provided when you opened your account, some accounts do not have grace periods and will charge a late fee or report your account as being late if payment is received on or after the due date. If you cannot find this information contact the company or go to their website to find out.

Be careful about going to a credit counseling agency or bankruptcy lawyer to help repair your credit. They promise to erase all your debts and make you believe you will have good credit after using their services. This is absolutely not true. They also claim to remove bankruptcies, judgments and delinquent loans. Many of the companies only want to make money and you will end up owing more money than if you just paid the bills on your own. Their promises are not true and they do not do anything special that you cannot do for yourself. They simply take the time to analyze the situation and call or write letters to get the matter resolved. You can do that yourself for free.

Many of these companies do not have to follow the same strict rules that creditors do and as a result many people lose their money or get further in debt by using these services. Most of these companies require you to pay money before any services are provided. They often neglect to inform you about your legal rights and how you can correct mistakes yourself.

They may suggest you get a new identity by applying for an employer identification number (EIN) and use this number instead of your social security number. This does not remove your bad credit with your social security number and will send a red flag to lenders especially if you do not have your own business. Further it can be illegal, causing you much bigger problems in the future. If you are caught by the IRS you can be fined or go to jail for providing a false social security number.

If a credit counseling agency promises that your credit will be repaired with a money back guarantee, many times this guarantee is not honored. Unfortunately, your social security number remains on file for as long as you live and whatever debts you made using your social security number, you will still owe. They also encourage you to dispute all negative information on your credit report, even information that is accurate. This is faulty logic, since you may be prosecuted for participating in any illegal activity that you were advised to do by the credit counseling agency such as obtaining an EIN.

Working with a credit counseling agency does not ensure that your credit will be repaired any quicker than doing it yourself. Be wary of companies that do rapid scoring or give a time limit on how soon your credit can be repaired. This can range from one month to several months to years depending on how accurate your records are and how fast the credit reporting agency can update the information.

Therefore, no company can accurately predict how soon your credit will be repaired. If you have been or are currently a customer of a credit counseling agency and feel you are not getting adequate service you may file a complaint with the FTC. You can also call your state Attorney General's Office of Consumer Affairs. You can contact the National Association of Consumer Advocates to get a referral for a lawyer at www.naca.net to explain your situation and get guidance on what your options are. However, this method will be expensive and should be your last resort.

Remember, if you fall behind in your payments follow these two tips to protect your credit:

- Notify your creditor(s) immediately and set up a payment plan. Some creditors participate in a debt repayment program which may charge a fee for this service.
- Some credit card companies have insurance that will automatically make payments on your account(s) until you are able to regain employment. Be sure to carefully read the agreement and assess your finances to ensure if you can afford to pay the associated fees.

While you are in the process of repairing your credit, remember:

- If a creditor continues to call you and is harassing you, inform them of your particular situation, get the person's name, date and time they called and tell them when you will be able to make a payment.
- Get a copy of your credit report at least once a year from the three major credit reporting agencies: Equifax, Experian and TransUnion.
- The quickest way to obtain your credit report is to order it online by going to www.annualcreditreport.com.

When writing letters to set up payment plans for delinquent accounts, remember to:

- Be honest, humble and sincere.
- Identify any terms and negotiations you would like to make.
- Stick to the terms in your letter.
- Reassure the company that it will not happen again and that you appreciate them doing business with you.

This chapter talked about how to begin repairing your credit. Although you are overwhelmed by your debt, don't be overwhelmed by the information provided in this chapter. The information will help you get out of debt and achieve financial freedom. Take one step at a time. Identify one or two tips you would like to use and then gradually work towards using some of the additional tips. It takes hard work and discipline to repair your credit, but it is definitely worth it.

When you have good credit, you have financial freedom to buy what you need and want, within your abilities to pay it off. When you have good credit you don't have to screen your calls or worry about creditors calling you at home or work asking when a payment will be sent. Your credit did not go bad in one day so you can not fix it in one day, one week or even one month. It takes time and patience, but the reward is great. The next chapter will discuss how to improve your credit rating.

Chapter 6 – How to Improve Your Credit Rating

Chapter 5 provided you with the detailed steps you need to take to improve your credit. Once all of your debts are paid, or the most delinquent accounts are paid, you must continue to repair your credit rating. Credit ratings can be negative and positive and indicate to creditors your ability to repay loans or accounts. If you have no debt but have negative credit ratings you still will not be able to obtain credit and will be considered a credit risk. This chapter will provide you with ways to improve your credit rating.

I learned the many different ways to improve my credit rating through trial and error and by working with my many creditors, who often provided me with valuable information. When you get into financial trouble the last thing you think about is paying your creditors because you are so concerned with paying necessary bills, car, insurance, mortgage, utilities, etc. You may completely forget about your creditors.

Some creditors have insurance that pays your bills if you lose your job or become ill. It is wise to sign up for disability insurance if your job offers it. Some companies also provide additional disability insurance, so talk to your benefits representative to find out all of your options. You can also do research on the internet and find out about various plans available if your job does not offer disability insurance.

If the credit status for an account on your credit report has a negative rating, i.e. R3, R9, I9, this may be corrected very easily. If you owe Discover $500 and pay them $166.67 a month on time for three months, this will prove to Discover that, although you fell behind on your payments in the past, you can now pay your bill on time. You can write the company and ask them to restore the status of your account back to the original rating, I1 or R1. It is always up to the company to approve your request. They may deny your request, but it is worth a try.

Don't move around too much. One red flag that creditors look for is lack of stability. Creditors hate to issue credit to people who move frequently, so don't apply for credit unless you've lived in your current residence for at least a year.

Creditors like stability. If you've been at the same job for 3 years and living in the same home for 4 years, you are considered a good credit risk with a verifiable address and income. Creditors also look at your debt–to–income ratio, savings, payment history, and assets, and may also look at your payment history for utility bills.

You can get rejected for credit simply because the creditor was unable to open the phone book or call the phone company to verify your address. The key to stability is living where you can afford the rent or mortgage, even if the neighborhood is not what you hoped for. If you are an angry, aggressive person whose behavior has been reported to the police, your behavior can be noted on your credit report by your landlord and this will portray you as non–creditworthy. How many banks do you think will lend money to someone who gets in trouble or has gotten in trouble with the police?

If you decide to obtain a new credit card, avoid getting a department store or gas card. The interest rates are higher than the average interest rate and it is best to pay for everything in cash. If you are applying for a credit card be sure that the credit card offers no annual fee, no over the limit fee and at least a 25–day grace period. The grace period gives you enough time to make a payment without having to worry about it being reported on your credit report if your payment is less than 30 days late. Read the terms of the credit card carefully and be aware of penalty and flexible interest rates or annual rates that increase, if you are charged fees for exceeding your credit limit or make a late payment. You have a better chance of being approved for a credit card or a loan if your debt–to–income ratio is under 20% which is excellent.

An acceptable rate is 28%, and a rate of 36% makes lenders and creditors nervous because you are seen as a high credit risk, in the event you lose your job, become sick or fall behind in payments. Mortgage lenders may approve you if your debt–to–income ratio is between 28% and 36%. If a lender approves you with a debt–to–income ratio higher than 36% you should be leery because chances are you will have to pay a higher interest rate, provide a larger down payment or may not be able to get the best terms possible.

Always pay more than the minimum monthly payment. If you send in the minimum payment every month, it could take over three years to pay off your balance, because interest is accruing on the remaining balance. Keep at least one creditor happy. If you're in serious debt and are considering filing for bankruptcy, or develop bad credit, stop charging for 6 months, and concentrate on keeping at least one of your credit accounts in good standing. Keep no more than 2 major credit cards and possibly one travel card, such as American Express, which forces you to pay the balance at the end of the month.

Remember the following six tips to prevent getting bad credit:

- Sign up for disability insurance if your job offers it.

- Always pay more than the minimum monthly payment. Since the minimum monthly payments for credit cards has doubled to 4% of the credit card balance, it may not be possible to pay the minimum monthly payment which is why it is necessary to keep good credit.

- Creditors like stability. Try your best to stay at each job for at least two years and stay at your residence for at least two years.

- Don't bounce checks.

- If you decide to obtain a new credit card, avoid getting a department store or gas card because the interest rates are higher than the average interest rate.

- Do your best to keep your debt–to–income ratio between 28% and 36% but try to aim for 28% or below.

This chapter informed you of how to improve your credit rating and prevent you from getting bad credit. Without good credit it is difficult to buy anything and even harder to get the best possible deal on interest rates and loans. When you have good credit you can negotiate with lenders and creditors to get the best deal because you are not seen as a credit risk and you've proven that you are able to handle your finances and keep your word to pay your bills on time each month. The next chapter will discuss how to keep good credit.

Chapter 7 – How to Keep Good Credit

The previous chapters provided the tools and techniques to repay your debts, repair your credit and restore your credit rating. This chapter will reinforce ways to keep good credit. Below are some ways to retain your good credit. This list is a result of things I learned while repairing my credit. I learned my lessons the hard way, but I am a better person for it. Now, I am passing this valuable information on to you, so you don't make the same mistakes I did which will help you to keep your good credit.

You may have seen some of these tips in other sections for improving your credit. They are listed here to remind you that, once your credit is better, you need to maintain many of these practices to keep it that way. Other tips listed here may be new to you. The list is long, so you may want to take several weeks before you begin to implement the whole list, focusing on a plan for implementing one or two at a time. Next to each item, you may want to prioritize which are most important to you to begin with right away, and which you will do in the next week or two. **Here are nineteen tips for keeping good credit:**

— Pay for everything in cash.

— Document all your debt and keep track of it until it is paid in full.

— Have only two or three credit cards and make sure they have a reasonable limit.

— Keep your balances at 50% or below the credit limit; but it is best if balances are kept at 30% or below the credit limit.

— If possible remain at your job and current residence for at least two years.

— Use your credit card for emergency purposes only.

— Have no more than a total of eleven open and closed accounts on your credit report.

— Make your payments on time, or early, each month in order to avoid late fees for overdue payments.

— Do not apply for a credit card by mail. This will result in unnecessary junk mail and additional offers for credit cards.

— Do not get advances from a credit card or employer.

— Do not borrow money from a 401(k); get a personal loan to pay off a debt.

— Budget your money and cut down on all unnecessary expenses.
— Don't use lack of knowledge about credit as an excuse for having bad credit.
— Open a savings account but do not open an account with a bank that you previously owed money to.
— Open a retirement account.
— Buy health, life and disability insurance.
— Purchase a home.
— When applying for a credit card remember that, if you fall behind in payments, the creditor may call you continually all times of the day and night to try to receive a payment.
— Consolidating student loans will get you a better interest rate but will appear as multiple accounts with multiple debts. The more debt accounts you have the lower your credit score will be.

Try to keep your credit card balances at fifty percent or below the credit limit because this will decrease your credit score because it is assumed that you cannot manage your money and pay your debts.

If you are a contractor, write each credit bureau agency and ask them to add a note to your credit report indicating that you are a contractor and you are given various short term assignments which requires you to work at many different locations. If you move because of your job, write each credit bureau agency and ask them to add a note to your credit report indicating that you have to move frequently because of your job (i.e. indicate if you are military employee, peace corp. employee, etc.). If you are on active military duty notify each credit bureau agency and ask them to update your status to "active duty alert".

Don't be alarmed if you have more than a total of eleven open and/or closed accounts on your credit report. Make sure that the open accounts are current and work to ensure any delinquent accounts become current. If you need extra money get a part–time job, gain extra skills by getting a degree or taking courses. Pay for gas and everything with cash. You may not be able to purchase health insurance, life insurance and disability insurance all at one time. Health insurance should be purchased first, followed by disability insurance. These two will ensure that if you become ill you will not go into debt due to your illness. If you own a home and your property value increases you will have equity in your home and this creates wealth. Also purchase homeowner's insurance to cover any property damage that may occur.

Credit card interest rates cause consumers to pay more than the original amount purchased on a credit card. Since you have repaired your credit using the steps in chapters one through six you need to continue to reduce expenses and one way is by paying your credit card balance in full each month. There are three different methods credit card companies use to calculate the finance charges. The most common method used to calculate finance charges is the average daily balance (ADB) method. Creditors must tell you when finance charges begin on your account and the method they use to figure the balance that you pay finance charges on. This information is called a consumer disclosure or disclosure which helps you compare costs and terms of various companies. This information must be provided based on the Truth In Lending laws that require creditors to provide consumers with information about the cost of buying on credit or taking out a loan.

The ADB gives you credit for your payment the same day the card issuer receives it. The ADB is the most commonly used method by creditors and is calculated by taking the daily balance on each day of the billing period or billing cycle minus any payments received, divided by the number of days in the billing period. Because of the way the ADB is calculated, **sending in your payment as early as possible will help you save money in interest charges**. The finance charge using the ADB method is calculated as follows:

ADB * Daily Periodic Rate * the number of days in the billing cycle = Monthly Finance Charge and let's say your ADB is $1000, your billing cycle is 31 days and your daily periodic rate is .03288%. = $1,000 * .03288% * 31 = $10.20 Monthly Finance Charge, so your total credit card balance for the month would be $1,000 + 10.20 = $1,010.20. This process is repeated each month until the balance is paid in full.

The other three methods used are the adjusted balance, previous balance and two cycle average daily balance. These methods are rarely used by credit card companies to calculate interest charges. The adjusted balance method is calculated by subtracting all payments made during the current period from the ending balance due from the last period. Purchases made during the period are not included in the computation. **The adjusted balance method is best for cardholders because it excludes purchases made during the current period and subtracts all payments made from the balance remaining from the last billing cycle**.

The previous balance method is computed by calculating finance charges based on the amount owed at the end of the last billing cycle. Payments, new purchases, etc. are excluded from the computation. This would result in a lower finance charge. However, most credit card companies, almost 100 percent in fact, use the adjusted daily balance method to calculate finance charges.

The two cycle average daily balance method uses the average daily balances for two billing cycles to compute the finance charge. Payments are subtracted to get the balance and new purchases may or may not be included in the computation.

When getting a loan or credit card take into consideration the finance charge, length of loan, and Annual Percentage Rate (APR). All banks, credit card companies and other companies have to state the cost of using their credit which includes specifying the finance charge and APR. If a company refuses to do this inform them that they are violating the Truth in Lending law and search for another company to do business with.

When filling out a credit card or loan application provide a voice mail or number other than your home telephone number to avoid harassing calls if you should fall behind in payments. Remember that when you provide your home telephone number on a credit or loan application this is sold to several other companies who wish to offer you their products or services. These calls usually appear as "out of area", "unavailable", "anonymous" or "private" on your caller id.

The more debt accounts you have as a result of multiple student loans you risk the chance of your credit score decreasing. Weigh your options when consolidating student loans. You can also contact the credit reporting agencies and ask for their advice about consolidating loans and how it will affect your credit score. Always check your monthly bills for errors. If you find an error on your bill, contact the company in writing and notify them of the problem. Contact the credit reporting agencies in writing and notify them that you are working with the creditor concerning a dispute with your account. Keep a log of all correspondence and telephone calls.

Don't let others use your credit cards. Don't get joint accounts unless you are married. **Get a copy of your credit report at least once a year and especially before making a large purchase such as a home or car.** You should always sign the back of your credit card. In the event your credit card is stolen and someone uses it, you can verify that the charges made were not by you based on a signature comparison.

To reduce the amount of junk mail you receive you can contact the Direct Marketing Association, at www.dmaconsumers.org or call 888–567–8688, and request that your name, address, and telephone number be omitted from telemarketer lists for five years or permanently. I opted to be removed from the telemarketer mailing lists permanently. To verify that your name and information has been removed, verify that the following text appears on your credit report: "File blocked for promotional purposes" or "File blocked for promotional purposes for five years" or some text similar to that. This will also prevent companies from making promotional inquiries which appear on your credit report and remain there for two years.

If you are applying for credit this appears on your credit report as an inquiry. If you have too many inquiries this can be held against if you are planning to apply for another credit card or make a large purchase, such as a car or home, because it is an indication of how much credit you are trying to obtain and lowers your credit score. If a lender sees too many inquiries they will assume you are trying to apply for too much credit and will not be a responsible credit user. They are likely to deny your request for credit. Reduce the number of inquiries by only applying for credit that you need not just because you received an offer for a pre–approved credit card or because you will get a discount for opening an account.

Most inquiries are done without your knowledge and this is all legal. Inquiries remain on your credit report for two years and should be removed automatically by the credit reporting agency. If the inquiry has not been removed by the two year period, contact the credit reporting agency and notify them that the inquiry should be removed. However, if you have done business with a company and you are notified that your credit report will be pulled and your credit report is pulled a second time, this is illegal. You should contact the company and tell them that an unauthorized inquiry was performed on your account and get a reason why this was done. Ask the company to remove the second unauthorized inquiry and notify you in writing when it has been removed. Also, write your local BBB and the FTC to file a complaint against the company.

If you are shopping around for the best deal, do research on the internet or on the telephone first without providing your personal information such as SSN, etc. You can call the company and provide general information and ask for a general quote. Ask for a fixed interest rate. Variable interest rates will cause you to pay more interest on the money owed when the interest rates increase and if you have good credit you can negotiate with your creditor to get a fixed interest rate. Do not allow the company to obtain your credit report unless you are absolutely sure you want to do business with the company.

You now have good credit and are able to effectively manage your money. Take caution when creditors increase your credit limit, always check your debt–to–income ratio. Contact the creditor if you wish to have your credit limit set back at the original limit if your debt–to–income–ratio is above 28%. Before making a large purchase check your credit limits against the amount of debt owed on each account. If you have a credit limit of $2,000 and you owe $1,500 you owe more than 50% of your credit limit which is a red flag to lenders that you might have bad spending habits which decreases your credit score.

There are many things you can do to keep good credit. **Here are thirteen tips for keeping your good credit.** You may want to post them somewhere you will see them often, such as your scheduling calendar, in your wallet or on your refrigerator.

— Pay for everything in cash.

— Keep your balances low by having only two or three credit cards with a reasonable limit.

— Use your credit card for emergency purposes only.

— Have no more than a total of eleven open and closed accounts on your credit report.

— Have a steady residence history and a steady work history.

— Make your payments on time or early each month in order to avoid late fees for overdue payments.

— Keep a credit score of at least 700.

— Do not get advances from a credit card or employer.

— Budget your money and cut down on all unnecessary expenses.

— Buy health, disability and life insurance.

— Purchase a home and homeowner's insurance to cover any property damage that may occur.

— Get a copy of your credit report at least once a year and especially before making a large purchase such as a home or car.

— If you are shopping around for the best deal for insurance, a car, or credit card interest rates, do research on the internet first before making a decision.

Chapter 7 discussed how to keep your good credit. The hardest part is getting good credit. With good habits, it's easy to keep it. Once you take my advice from the previous chapters you should be well on your way to getting good credit and will soon be able to shout for joy when you become debt free. These seven chapters will ensure that you are able to repair your credit yourself and obtain good credit all on your own using this book as your guide. The following chapter discusses specific information about credit and your credit rights.

Chapter 8 – General Information About Your Credit

This chapter will discuss some basic information you need to know about your credit and your credit rights. **You must provide consent (usually by filling out a form and signing it) for a company to obtain your credit report.** A credit reporting agency can not give out information about you to your employer or prospective employer without your written consent and cannot report medical information about you to creditors without your permission.

If anyone asks for a copy of your credit report, be sure to ask why they need this information. If it is for a job and you have poor credit, be prepared to provide documentation or an explanation of why you have poor credit. If the credit report is for a job, you can ask the employer to provide you with a copy of the credit report. If you are declined a job because of your credit, you can ask the employer to provide you with the credit reporting agency that declined you and obtain a free copy of your credit report. It is a good idea to get a copy of your credit report *before* applying for a job or making a large purchase, such as a home or car, so that if anything negative is on the report you are not surprised if you have difficulty obtaining a loan or getting approved for credit. You should begin immediately to try to repair your credit.

Some employers use your credit report as a means to determine if you are a trustworthy person. If you have a negative credit report, this information can be used against you without your knowledge. If you feel the information on your credit report was used against you, notify the company that they must tell you the reason why it was used against you, tell them to give you the name, address and telephone number of the credit reporting agency that provided the credit report.

One way to reduce errors on your credit report is by using the same name every time you fill out an application unless you have gotten married. Always specify suffix if you are a junior, senior, or III. The following information is listed on your credit report and you may request that it be updated at any time:

- Name and any alias (other) names used
- SSN (social security number)
- DOB (date of birth)

- Current address plus the two most recent previous addresses
- Current employer's name plus the two most recent previous employer's names
- Home telephone number

Data is reported on your credit report for accounts such as bank cards, department stores, travel and entertainment cards such as American Express or Diners club card and federal student loans. Data for the following accounts are usually not reported on your credit report unless you have been delinquent: utility bills, medical bills, and rent.

Debt collectors must identify themselves when they call you. Debt collectors cannot harass anyone nor use threats, violence or harm, use profane language or telephone you all hours of the day or night. Debt collectors must identify themselves when calling to collect a debt owed. If you are a victim of this behavior, contact the FTC at 877–FTC–HELP, or online at www.ftc.gov to file a complaint. Debt collectors cannot make false statements, imply that they are attorneys or that you have committed a crime, (it is not against the law to have bad credit), increase the amount you owe, or indicate that they will sue you by sending legal papers. Remember to keep all documents your creditors send you and keep a copy of all documents you send to your creditors.

Debt collectors cannot: place calls without the disclosure of the caller's identity, call you collect, come to your job or home without written consent from you, contact you by postcard, threaten you, make your debts public except to a credit reporting agency, contact a relative or friend to try to get information about your debt, however a creditor can contact a friend or relative to get your contact information. To stop this from happening, write the creditor or collection agency and tell them to stop harassing you. Send the letter by certified mail and request a signature when the letter is delivered. Once the creditor or collection agency receives your letter they may not contact you again unless they notify you that they intend to take action against you.

Remember, if a creditor or collection agency continues to call you, inform them of your particular situation, get the person's name, date and time they called and tell them when you will be able to make a payment. If they continue to call you after that, inform them that you will report them to the FTC Consumer Response Center for harassment, and that you can sue them in court for violation of the FCRA.

The following information is listed on your credit report and you may request that it be updated at any time if it is incorrect:

- Name and any alias (other) names used
- SSN (social security number)

- DOB (date of birth)
- Current address plus the two most recent previous addresses
- Current employer's name plus the two most recent previous employer's names
- Home telephone number

Here are three tips to remember about your credit:
- You must provide consent (usually by filling out a form and signing it) for a company to obtain your credit report.
- Data is reported on your credit report for accounts such as bank cards, department stores, travel and entertainment cards such as American Express or Diners club cards and federal student loans.
- Data for the following accounts are usually not reported on your credit report unless you have been delinquent: utility bills, medical bills, and rent.

Creditors treat consumers with bad credit like they are criminals and use all kinds of intimidation and tricks to force people to pay their debts. To force creditors to change their behavior consumers: must file complaints against creditors when they have a problem, write their congressman and inform them that creditors have too much power, that it is not a crime to have bad credit, and that creditors should be fined if they harass consumers with bad credit. Often, both consumer and creditor are responsible for the situation: if a person has bad credit and a credit company approves them for additional credit, the company takes some responsibility for approving credit to someone who already had financial troubles.

This chapter explained general information about credit, rights you have as a consumer and identified ways to protect yourself from creditors harassing you. If you don't have bad credit then you won't have to worry about annoying creditors calling you requesting payment. The next chapter discusses how to deal with telemarketers and creditors.

Chapter 9 – How to Deal with Telemarketers and Creditors

This chapter provides ways to deal with creditors and telemarketers. You know the scenario: you are relaxing at home one evening, get out of your comfy chair to answer the telephone and hear a recording tell you about a product for you to purchase. Most of us hate telemarketers and have done all kinds of things to avoid their calls such as purchasing caller id, screening our calls, purchasing call intercept, etc. You as a consumer have several rights that you may not know about.

To assist with eliminating or reducing telemarketer calls, purchase caller id if you can afford it. Also, go to www.dmaconsumers.org and request that you are opted out of promotional advertisements. You can opt out for mail and phone calls for good or for a period of five years. I opted out for good and rarely receive telemarketer calls or junk mail. When I do receive junk mail I immediately call the company or write them a letter stating that I wish to be removed from their mailing list, telephone lists (if they have your telephone number) and all third party mailing lists and I ask when it will be effective. I suggest you do the same. If they say it should be effective in a few weeks, be persistent and request that it be effective immediately. Be sure to ask for the person's name when you speak with them in case you continue to receive junk mail from that company in the future. In some instances companies continue to send you junk mail.

This happened to me and after calling the company three times, I filled a complaint with the BBB and reported the company to the FTC informing them that I had requested to be removed from their mailing lists three times and continued to receive junk mail. Finally, I stopped receiving junk mail from that company.

If you don't mind receiving junk mail then you don't have to opt out. However, consider this: with the increase in identify theft, a situation where someone goes through your mail or obtains your personal information and uses information they find to "steal" your identity, someone can go through your mail, find an offer for a pre–approved credit card and use that credit card in your name. You would never know until you obtained your credit report. Also, once you start receiving junk mail your name and address are sold to many companies and these companies also send junk mail. If you want to obtain a credit card, go to the store or call the company and ask to be sent an application. That way you know exactly who you are doing business with. Don't throw junk mail addressed to you directly in the trash. Open the junk mail and tear up portion with your name, address, or any other personal information on it to reduce your chances of becoming a victim of identity theft.

If a telemarketer repeatedly calls you at home or at work, inform them that you are not interested in buying any of their products or services and request that your name be removed from their database or contact lists. Many times calls are made by computer and once the computer registers that a person answered the call, the system will continue to call until they get a response. If they get no answer they may wait two or three weeks and start the process all over again. Dealing with telemarketers depends on your communication style. If you don't mind talking to them then you should answer the telephone, but remember, if you answer the telephone, your phone number will be registered as a valid number that will be sold to thousands of other companies that will try to sell you products.

Another way to prevent telemarketers from calling you is by using a service that Verizon has called "call intercept." This forces a person to identify themselves if their telephone number appears as "out of area", "unavailable", "anonymous" or "private" on your caller id. If the person refuses to identify themselves, the call will not go through. You can purchase caller id and call intercept from your local telephone company. Since telemarketer numbers usually appear as "out of area", "unavailable", "anonymous" or "private" you will know to avoid answering these phone calls.

According to the Fair and Debt Collection Practices Act (FDCPA) creditors cannot harass you, hang up on you, make repeated calls, cannot contact anyone other than you to collect a debt (but can contact others to get your address, phone number or place of employment), cannot call before 8 a.m. or after 9 p.m., cannot ask you to pay the debt using a post–dated check for more than five days after current date. If they do receive a post–dated check for more than five days after the current date they must notify you in writing that they will deposit the check. They cannot use profanity, threats or violence to obtain the debt owed. They must be honest with you at all times. If you feel you are being harassed have a friend or family member listen on the phone during your conversation or listen to the answering machine message that was left.

Contact the collection agency or creditor and notify them that you have evidence of harassment and indicate that they are violating the FDCPA. If you do not get any response from the collection agency you can contact the original creditor or file a complaint with the FTC and your local BBB.

Beware of lenders or creditors who "guarantee" that you will be approved for a car, loan or home. No one can "guarantee" that you will be approved because the method for determining approval is a very complex mathematical process that cannot be predetermined without documentation.

This chapter explained ways to deal with creditors and telemarketers calling your home. There are several things you can do such as educate yourself about your credit rights and pay your debts as soon as possible, but the main thing is that any time you fill out an application or form that asks for your personal information, you are essentially saying that thousands of companies can use your information to send you junk mail or call your home to ask you to buy goods or services. You should only fill out an application when you are sure you are about to buy something and not just fill out forms to win a contest or for a survey. You also don't know what is going to be done with your information or how your information is protected and stored. This is a serious risk to your personal security and could increase your chances of identity theft, which is discussed in the following chapter.

Chapter 10 – Identity Theft

This chapter discusses a new threat to consumers, identity theft, and how to protect yourself before or after it happens. Identity theft is a new crime in which one's identity is stolen. A person will steal one's identity by using your name, driver's license, social security number, address, telephone number, receipts, bank statements, credit card, etc. and apply for credit or loans, make purchases, rent cars, cash checks, apply for jobs, buy gasoline or open new accounts in your name.

Unfortunately, some people don't know that their identity is stolen or don't find out until it is too late. To reduce the risk of identity theft, whenever you are asked for your personal information, ask why your personal information is needed and what will be done with it. Also ask, "Once I am no longer a customer of this company, what will be done with my information and how it will be destroyed?" If you prefer, ask for your personal records so that you may destroy them yourself. The company may not agree to this but it is worth a try.

I was a victim of identity theft. I rented a car and had to fax the representative back my credit card information. I faxed it when he was not in the office. As a result, my identity was stolen and my credit card was charged with purchases.

Luckily I didn't have a large amount left on my credit card to charge with. The identity thieves also tried to buy gas but were unable to. I had to go through a long process to fill out forms, provide my signature and write a statement indicating that I did not make the purchases. Luckily I was not charged for the purchases and they were able to track down the thieves. Afterwards I put a fraud alert on my credit card account and still have it on my account. If you are or have been a victim of identity theft contact the three major credit reporting agencies and ask for an extended seven year fraud alert on your credit file. You will be notified every time a new account is opened or an item is charged to ensure that you are aware of all transactions on your credit card accounts. You can also ask about getting a security freeze on your account.

Here are nineteen tips to help you protect your identity.

— Obtain a copy of your credit report once a year and verify that all the information on the report is correct.

— Make copies of all of your identification cards and credit cards and store in a safe place.

— Shred any credit card application, or any documents with your personal information, instead of throwing them directly in the trash.

— When throwing away shredded documents put them in a secure trash bag and preferably mixed in with other trash so the documents cannot be easily seen by someone if the trash bag is picked up.

— Review your monthly statements for accuracy.

— Use a post office box or locked mailbox for incoming and outgoing mail.

— When ordering checks make sure they can be delivered in a secure mailbox, if not have them delivered to a friend or relative's home.

— Avoid giving out your social security number unless it is absolutely necessary for a line of credit, bank, lender, tax form, etc.

— Save your ATM, debit card, check card and credit card receipts and verify them against your monthly statements.

— Sign the back of your credit card to prevent someone else from signing it.
— If you must purchase an item online, be sure that the company is reputable.
— Secure passwords, PINs and account numbers, and use a different password or PIN for each of your accounts.
— Keep track of when your monthly bills and bank or asset statements should arrive in the mail, notify companies when you have not received your bills, ask to receive another copy, and verify your mailing address.
— Purchase a safe deposit box or fireproof safe to keep in your home to store personal papers and information.
— Do not carry your credit cards in your wallet unless you are definitely going to use them. If you must carry a credit card in your wallet, carry only one.
— Don't carry personal papers, bills, passwords or personal information in your wallet or purse, i.e. passwords, pin numbers, receipts, birth certificate, social security number, etc.
— When doing business with a company find out what their security policies are, how your personal information is stored and opt out of their advertising and third party mailings.
— Reduce the amount of business conducted over the internet such as online shopping and banking.

— If you are working out of the country on a temporary assignment notify the three credit reporting agencies and ask them to add a note to your credit report and include in the note when your temporary assignment will end.

Make copies of all of your credit cards and identification cards – the front and back so that, in the event your cards are lost, stolen or used, you can use the copies as proof of your signature. Try to keep at least a year's worth of your statements, which may come in handy for future reference. When you order checks through the mail never have the mailman leave them at your door. Also, don't include your home telephone number when ordering checks, use a work or cell phone number which cannot be as easily traced back to you. Only give out your social security number if you feel comfortable doing so, you don't have to give out your social security number when making purchases or filling out background information such as with a doctor or dentist although you may be told that you do. Don't carry your social security card or birth certificate in your wallet because, if your wallet is stolen, so is your identity.

When purchasing something online you can check out the company by going to the BBB website and viewing a report on the company at www.bbb.org. Ensure the website is secure when you are ready to purchase an item online. Secure links start with "https://." Also ensure that a lock symbol appears in the lower right hand corner of the screen to indicate the website is secure, or you may also see a company logo such as Verisign that indicates the website is secure. Also, don't let the website store your username, password, address or credit card information for future use. This may make it easier for you the next time you make a purchase but increases your risk of being a victim of identity theft. Some companies automatically store this information so access your account to delete your personal information.

Choose passwords that contain letters and numbers and never use your birth date, social security number, name, or anything that attaches the password to you. If you monthly bills or asset statements don't arrive in the mail and this occurs more than once or twice, call the company to find out if they have the correct address or contact your post office to see why you are not receiving all of your mail. Don't take mail to work or carry mail, especially bills, with you. Keep all of your mail at home in a private place (not where guests can see them). Keep PIN's, passwords, etc. in a safe and secure place at home.

Also, ask if you can add a password to your bank and credit card accounts to prevent unauthorized access. If you do business over the internet such as shopping or banking do business with the same company, for example if you have multiple bank accounts at various banks don't use online banking for all of your accounts. If you do online shopping buy products from one company. Make sure it is a secure trusted website. Your chances of online identity theft are less when you do less activity over the internet. No one method is 100% secure (online or not online) but try to reduce your chances of being a victim.

If you are a military employee that is on active duty you can call the three credit reporting agencies and ask to put an "active duty alert" on your credit report to reduce chances of identity theft.

If you become a victim of identity theft or a mugging, notify your creditors and close all of your accounts. Also notify the creditor reporting agencies immediately and ask them to enter a fraud alert and security freeze on your credit file which can prevent new accounts from being opened in your name. Also file a police report and be persistent if the police refuse to file a report for you. Send documents registered or certified mail and keep records of everyone you speak to. Contact your local Social Security Administration, department of motor vehicles, post office, and passport agency and notify them you were a victim of identity theft. Also follow up all conversations with a letter confirming what was said in the conversation. You can also notify the Human Resources Department at your job to ask them not to give out your personal information without your permission. Also notify your bank, mortgage, check registry companies, and all other companies that you have an account with and inform them that you have been a victim of identity fraud.

Close any accounts that have been accessed and open new accounts with new PINs or passwords. Create PINs and passwords that cannot be easily guessed, try to use a combination of letters and numbers, don't use your social security number, birth date, middle names, spouse or children's names, or address. Go to your local post office and request a change of address form. Change your mailing address to a friend or relative's address or obtain a post office box.

To reduce chances of becoming a victim of identity theft purchase a paper shedder and use this to shred all personal documents that you plan to throw away. Put the shredded paper in secured trash bags that are not clear or see–through. Also, don't place papers with personal information in the recycle bins. Thieves rummage through trash and recycle bins to obtain old bank statements and credit card statements to steal a person's identity. Don't give out personal information over the phone, via the mail or internet unless you are sure you are doing business with a trustworthy company.

Remove mail everyday from your mailbox and put your mail on hold when you go on vacation. Don't carry your social security card or birth certificate in your purse or wallet. Don't store personal information on a computer or laptop at work.

Each time you fill out an application or apply for credit remember, you are allowing your personal information to be seen and handled by several people. Before applying for credit ask the company what their privacy policy is, how consumer information is stored, where it is stored and what steps they take in the event a consumer is a victim of identity theft or the company data is compromised by hackers or a virus. Once you have more knowledge about privacy policies and security measures you will be able to make a better decision about what companies you do business with. You can also do research on the internet about various companies and their track records by going to the BBB website at www.bbb.org.

This chapter explored identity theft and ways to reduce your risk of being a victim, as well as what to do if you become a victim. Unfortunately, the world today is full of criminals and scam artists who prey on people with bad credit who are so desperate to get out of debt they agree to almost anything in the hopes repairing their credit and paying their debts.

Conclusion

Debt keeps you in bondage. You will have a much happier life when your debt becomes manageable or totally eliminated. I hope this book helps you get out of debt no matter what your financial situation – whether you're single, divorced, separated, widowed, unemployed, underemployed, married or a student. I wish I had someone who could have provided me with this advice: I would have saved thousands of dollars, time, stress and headaches. I know you have the ability to repair your credit on your own and be debt free like I am. Now it's up to you. Good luck to you and I wish you financial success!

Appendix A – Consumer Protection Agencies and State Resources

This appendix contains lists for agencies that can assist consumers with disputes, harassment, and provide assistance related to credit problems and debt.

Associated Credit Bureaus Inc (provides free brochures on credit bureaus and the Fair Credit Reporting Act)
1090 Vermont Avenue, NW, Suite 200
Washington, DC 20005

Federal Trade Commission
Division of Credit Practices
600 Penn. Avenue, N.W.
Washington, DC 20580
www.ftc.gov/bcp/bcpcp.htm

State Agencies
Alabama
Consumer Affairs Section
Office of the Attorney General
11 South Union St.
Montgomery, AL 36130
334–242–7335
Toll free in AL: 1–800–392–5658
www.ago.state.al.us

State Banking Authorities
Superintendent of Banks
Center for Commerce
Suite 689
401 Adams Ave.
Montgomery, AL 36130–1201
334–242–3452
Fax: 334–242–3500
www.bank.state.al.us

State Insurance Regulators

Department of Insurance
201 Monroe St.
Suite 1700
PO Box 303351
Montgomery, AL 36104
334–269–3550
Fax: 334–241–4192
Email:
insdept@insurance.state.al.us
www.aldoi.org

State Securities Administrators
Securities Commission
770 Washington Ave.
Suite 570
Montgomery, AL 36130–4700
334–242–2984
Toll free in AL: 1–800–222–1253
Fax: 334–242–0240
Email: asc@asc.alabama.gov
asc.state.al.us/

State Utility Commissions
Public Service Commission
PO Box 304260
Montgomery, AL 36130
Toll free in AL: 1–800–392–8050
Fax: 334–242–0727
www.psc.state.al.us

Alaska
Consumer Protection Unit
Office of the Attorney General
1031 West 4th Ave., Suite 200

Anchorage, AK 99501–5903
907–269–5100
Fax: 907–276–8554
www.law.state.ak.us

State Banking Authorities
Division of Banking and
Securities
Department of Commerce,
Community
and Economic Development
P.O. Box 11807
Juneau, AK 99811–0807
907–465–2521
TDD: 907–465–5437
Fax: 907–465–2549
Email: dbsc@dced.state.ak.us
www.dced.state.ak.us/bsc/bsc
.htm

State Insurance Regulators
Department of Commerce,
Community and Economic
Development
PO Box 110805
Juneau, AK 99811–0805
907–465–2515
TDD/TTY: 907–465–5437
Fax: 907–465–3422
Email:
insurance@commerce.state.ak.
us
www.commerce.state.ak.us/in
surance/

Division of Insurance
Department of Commerce,

Community and Economic
Development
Robert B. Atwood Building
550 W. 7th Avenue
Suite 1560
Anchorage, AK 995013567
907–269–7900
TDD: 907–465–5437
Fax: 907–269–7910
Email:
insurance@commerce.state.ak.
us
www.dced.state.ak.us/insuran
ce

**State Securities
Administrators**
Division of Banking and
Securities
Department of Commerce,
Community and Economic
Development
PO Box 11807
Juneau, AK 99811–0807
907–465–2521
TDD: 907–465–5437
Fax: 907–465–2549
www.dced.state.ak.us/bsc/bsc
.htm

State Utility Commissions
Regulatory Commission of
Alaska
701 W 8th Ave.
Suite 300
Anchorage, AK 99501
907–276–6222

TDD: 907–276–4533
Toll free in AK: 1–800–390–
2782
Fax: 907–276–0160
Email: cp_rca@rca.state.ak.us
www.state.ak.us/rca

Arizona
Consumer Protection and
Advocacy Section
Office of the Attorney General
1275 West Washington St.
Phoenix, AZ 85007
602–542–3702/602–542–5763
(Consumer Information and
Complaints)
Toll free in AZ: 1–800–352–
8431
TDD: 602–542–5002
Fax: 602–542–4579
www.azag.gov

Consumer Protection
Office of the Attorney General
400 West Congress South
Bldg., Suite 315
Tucson, AZ 85701
520–628–6504
Toll free in AZ: 1–800–352–
8431
Fax: 520–628–6532
www.azag.gov

State Banking Authorities
State Banking Department
2910 North 44th St.

Suite 310
Phoenix, AZ 85018
602–255–4421
Toll free in AZ: 1–800–544–
0708
Fax: 602–381–1225
www.azbanking.com

State Insurance Regulators
Department of Insurance
2910 North 44th St.
Suite 210
Phoenix, AZ 85018–7256
602–912–8444
Toll free in AZ: 1–800–325–
2548
Fax: 602–954–7008
(Complaints)
Email:
consumers@id.state.az.us
www.id.state.az.us

**State Securities
Administrators**
Securities Division
Arizona Corporation
Commission
1300 West Washington
3rd Fl
Phoenix, AZ 85007
602–542–4242
Fax: 602–594–7470
Email:
accsec@ccsd.cc.state.az.us
www.ccsd.cc.state.az.us

State Utility Commissions

144

Arizona Corporation
Commission
1200 West Washington St.
Phoenix, AZ 85007
602–542–3933
Toll free in AZ: 1–800–222–7000
TDD: 602–542–2105
Fax: 602–542–5560
Email:
mailmaster@cc.state.az.us
www.cc.state.az.us

Arkansas
Consumer Protection Division
Office of the Attorney General
323 Center St.
Suite 200
Little Rock, AR 72201
501–682–2007/501–682–2341
(Consumer Hotline)
Toll free: 1–800–482–8982 (Do
Not Call Program)
1–877–866–8225 (In–State Do
Not Call Program)
Toll free: 1–800–448–3014
(Crime Victims Hotline TDD:
501–682–6073)
Fax: 501–682–8118
Email:
consumer@ag.state.ar.us
www.ag.state.ar.us

State Banking Authorities
State Bank Department
400 Hardin Rd.

Suite 100
Little Rock, AR 72211
501–324–9019
Fax: 501–324–9028
Email:
asbd@banking.state.ar.us
www.accessarkansas.org/bank

State Insurance Regulators
Department of Insurance
1200 West 3rd St.
Little Rock, AR 72201–1904
501–371–2600/
501–371–2640 (Consumer
Services)
Toll free in AR: 1–800–282–9134
Toll free: 1–800–852–5494
Fax: 501–371–2618
Email:
insurance.consumers@arkansas.gov
www.arkansas.gov/insurance

State Securities Administrators
Securities Division
Heritage West Bldg.
Suite 300
201 East Markham
Little Rock, AR 72201
501–324–9260
Toll free: 1–800–981–4429
Toll free in AR: 1–800–981–4429

Fax: 501–324–9268
Email:
securities@mail.state.ar.us
www.arkansas.gov/arsec/

State Utility Commissions
Public Service Commission
PO Box 400
Little Rock, AR 72203–0400
501–682–2051
Toll free in AR: 1–800–482–
1164 (complaints)
TDD toll free: 800–682–2898
Fax: 501–682–5731
www.state.ar.us/psc

California
Office of the Attorney General
Public Inquiry Unit
P.O. Box 944255
Sacramento, CA 94244–2550
916–322–3360
Toll free in CA: 1–800–952–
5225
TDD: 916–324–5564
Fax: 916–323–5341
www.caag.state.ca.us

California Department of
Consumer Affairs
400 R St., Suite 1080
Sacramento, CA 95814
916–445–1254/916–445–4465
916–445–2643
(Correspondence and
Complaint Review Unit)
Toll free in CA: 1–800–952–

5210
TDD/TTY: 916–322–1700
Email: dca@dca.ca.gov
www.dca.ca.gov

State Banking Authorities
State Department of Financial
Institutions
111 Pine St., Suite 1100
San Francisco, CA 94111
415–263–8555
Toll free in CA: 1–800–622–
0620 (for consumer
complaints against CA state–
licensed banks
Fax: 415–989–5310
Email: consumer@dfi.ca.gov
www.dfi.ca.gov

State Insurance Regulators
Department of Insurance
300 Capitol Mall, Suite 1500
Sacramento, CA 95814
916–492–3500
415–538–4010 (San Francisco)
213–897–8921 (Los Angeles)
Toll free in CA: 1–800–927–
4357
Fax: 916–445–5280
www.insurance.ca.gov

Dept. of Managed Health
Care, California HMO Help
Center
(We serve all California
Consumers that are enrolled

in a California HMO, Blue Cross of California PPO, and Blue Shield of California PPO) 980 Ninth Street, Suite 500 Sacramento, CA 95814–2738 1–888–HMO–2219 (HMO Health Center Consumer Complaint Line) 1–877–525–1295 (HMO Help Center Provider/Physician Line) 1–877–688–9891 Fax: 916–229–0465 (Complaints) or (916) 229–4328 (Independent Medical Review) Email: GenInfo@dmhc.ca.gov www.hmohelp.ca.gov

State Securities Administrators
Department of Corporations 1515 K St., Suite 200 Sacramento, CA 95814–4052 916–445–7205 www.corp.ca.gov

State Utility Commissions
Public Utilities Commission 505 Van Ness Ave., Room 5218 San Francisco, CA 94102 415–703–2782 Toll free in CA: 1–800–649–7570 (Utility Complaints) TDD: 415–703–2032

Fax: 415–703–1758 www.cpuc.ca.gov/

Colorado
Consumer Protection Division Colorado Attorney General's Office 1525 Sherman St. 5th Floor Denver, CO 80203–1760 303–866–5079 Toll free: 1–800–222–4444 Fax: 303–866–5443

State Banking Authorities
Division of Banking Department of Regulatory Agencies 1560 Broadway, Suite 1175 Denver, CO 80202 303–894–7575 Fax: 303–894–7570 Email: banking@dora.state.co.us www.dora.state.co.us/banking/

State Insurance Regulators
Division of Insurance 1560 Broadway, Suite 850 Denver, CO 80202 303–894–7490 or 7499 Toll free in CO: 1–800–930–3745 TDD/TTY: 303–894–7880 Fax: 303–894–7455

www.dora.state.co.us/Insurance

State Securities Administrators
Division of Securities
Department of Regulatory
Agencies
1580 Lincoln St., Suite 420
Denver, CO 80203–1506
303–894–2320
TTY 1–800–659–2656
Fax: 303–861–2126
Email:
securities@dora.state.co.us
www.dora.state.co.us/securities

State Utility Commissions
Public Utilities Commission
1580 Logan St., Office Level 2
Denver, CO 80203
303–894–2070
Toll free in CO: 1–800–456–0855
TDD: 303–894–2512
Fax: 303–894–2065
Email:
PUConsumer.Complaints@dora.state.co.us
www.dora.state.co.us/puc/

Connecticut
Department of Consumer
Protection
165 Capitol Ave.

Hartford, CT 06106
860–713–6050
Fax: 860–713–7243
www.ct.gov/dcp

State Banking Authorities
Connecticut Department of
Banking
260 Constitution Plaza
Hartford, CT 06103
860–240–8200
Toll free in CT: 1–800–831–7225
Fax: 860–240–8178
www.state.ct.us/dob

State Insurance Regulators
Department of Insurance
Consumer Affairs Dept.
PO Box 816
Hartford, CT 06142–0816
860–297–3900
Toll free: 1–800–203–3447
Fax: 203–297–3872
www.state.ct.us/cid

State Securities Administrators
Department of Banking
Government Relations and
Consumer Affairs
260 Constitution Plaza
Hartford, CT 06103–1800
860–240–8299
Toll free: 1–800–831–7225
Fax: 860–240–8178
Email:

banking.complaints@po.state.
ct.us
www.state.ct.us/dob

State Utility Commissions
Department of Public Utility
Control
10 Franklin Square
New Britain, CT 06051
860–827–1553
Toll free in CT: 1–800–382–
4586
TDD: 860–827–2837
Fax: 860–827–2613
www.state.ct.us/dpuc/

Delaware
Fraud and Consumer
Protection Division
Office of the Attorney General
Carvel State Office Building
820 North French St., 5th
Floor
Wilmington, DE 19801
302–577–8600
Toll free in DE: 1–800–220–
5424
TTY: 302–577–6499
Fax: 302–577–2496
Email:
Attorney.General@State.DE.U
S
www.state.de.us/attgen/

State Banking Authorities
Office of the State Bank
Commissioner

555 East Lockerman St., Suite
210
Dover, DE 19901
302–739–4235
Fax: 302–739–2356
Email: choffecker@state.de.us
www.state.de.us/bank

State Insurance Regulators
Department of Insurance
841 Silver Lake Blvd.
Dover, DE 19904
302–739–4251
Toll free in DE: 1–800–282–
8611
Fax: Fax: 302–739–6278
Email:
consumer@deins.state.de.us
www.state.de.us/inscom

State Securities
Administrators
Division of Securities
Department of Justice
State Office Bldg.
820 North French St., 5th
Floor
Wilmington, DE 19801
302–577–8424
Fax: 302–577–6987
www.state.de.us/securities

State Utility Commissions
Public Service Commission
Cannon Bldg. Suite 100
861 Silver Lake Blvd.

Dover, DE 19904
302–739–4247
Toll free in DE: 1–800–282–8574
TDD: 302–739–4333
Fax: 302–739–4849
www.state.de.us/delpsc

District of Columbia
Consumer & Trade Protection Section
Office of the Attorney General for the District of Columbia
441 4th St., NW, Suite 450 N
Washington, DC 20001
202–442–9828
Fax: 202–727–6546
Email: consumercomplaint.occ@dc.gov

Department of Consumer and Regulatory Affairs
Government of the District of Columbia
941 North Capitol St., NE
Washington, DC 20002
202–442–4400
Citywide Call Center: 202–727–1000
Fax: 202–442–9445
Email: dcra@dc.gov
dcra.dc.gov

State Banking Authorities
Department of Insurance,
Securities and Banking

1400 L St., NW
Washington, DC 20005
202–727–1563
Fax: 202–727–1290
www.dbfi.dc.gov

State Insurance Regulators
Department of Insurance,
Securities and Banking
810 First St., NE, Suite 701
Washington, DC 20002
202–727–8000
Fax: 202–535–1196
Email: info.disb@dcgov.org
disb.dc.gov

State Securities Administrators
Dept. of Insurance, Securities and Banking
810 First St., NE, Suite 701
Washington, DC 20002
202–727–8000
Fax: 202–535–1196
Email: disb@dcgov.org
disb.dc.gov

State Utility Commissions
Public Service Commission
1333 H Street, NW
Suite 200, West Tower;
Washington, DC 20005
202–626–5100 (Consumer Services Division)
Fax: 202–393–1389
Email: support@dcpsc.org
www.dcpsc.org

Florida
Multi–State Litigation and
Intergovernmental Affairs
Office of the Attorney General
PL–01 The Capitol
Tallahassee, FL 32399
850–414–3300
Toll free in FL: 1–866–966–7226
Fax: 850–410–2672
myfloridalegal.com

Economic Crimes Division
Office of the Attorney General
PL–01 The Capitol
Tallahassee, FL 32399
850–414–3600
Toll free in FL: 1–866–966–7226
TDD toll free: 1–800–955–8771
Fax: 850–488–4483
myfloridalegal.com

Florida Dept. of Agriculture
and Consumer Service
2005 Apalachee Parkway
Tallahassee, FL 32399–6500
850–922–2966
(Toll free in FL only): 1–800–435–7352
Fax: 850–410–3839
www.800helpfla.com

Regional Offices
Economic Crimes Division
Office of the Attorney General
110 SE 6th St.

Fort Lauderdale, FL 33301–5000
954–712–4600
Fax: 954–712–4658

Economic Crimes Division
Office of the Attorney General
135 West Central Blvd., Suite 1000
Orlando, FL 32801
407–999–5588/Fax: 407–245–0365
myfloridalegal.com

Economic Crimes Division
Office of the Attorney General
Concourse Center 4
3507 E. Frontage Rd.
Suite 325
Tampa, FL 33607–1795
813–287–7950
Fax: 813–281–5515

Economic Crimes Division
Office of the Attorney General
1515 N. Flagler Ave., Suite 900
West Palm Beach, FL 33401
561–837–5000
Fax: 561–837–5109

State Banking Authorities
Department of Financial
Services
200 East Gaines St.
Tallahassee, FL 323990300

850–413–3100
Toll free in FL: 1–800–342–2762
TDD: 850–410–9700
Fax: 850–488–2349
www.fldfs.com

State Insurance Regulators
Office of Insurance Regulation
Department of Financial
Services
200 East Gaines St.
Tallahassee, FL 32399–0300
(850) 413–3100
Toll free in FL: 1–800–342–2762
TDD: 850–410–9700
Fax: 850–488–2349
www.fldfs.com

State Securities Administrators
Office of Financial Regulation
200 East Gaines St.
Tallahassee, FL 32399–0350
850–410–9805
Toll free in FL: 1–800–342–2762
Fax: 850–410–9748
Email: fldbf@dfs.state.fl.us
www.fldfs.com

State Utility Commissions
Florida Public Service
Commission
2540 Shumard Oak Blvd.
Tallahassee, FL 32399–0850

850–413–6330
Toll free in FL: 1–800–342–3552
TDD/TTY toll free: 1–800–955–8771
Fax: 800–511–0809
Email: contact@psc.state.fl.us
www.floridapsc.com

Georgia
Consumer Protection Agency
Governor's Office of
Consumer Affairs
2 Martin Luther King, Jr. Dr.,
Ste. 356
Atlanta, GA 30334
404–656–3790
Toll free in GA (outside
Atlanta area): 1–800–869–1123
Fax: 404–651–9018
www2.state.ga.us/gaoca

State Banking Authorities
Department of Banking and
Finance
2990 Brandywine Rd., Suite
200
Atlanta, GA 30341–5565
770–986–1653
Toll free in GA: (888) 986–1633
Fax: 770–986–1654
www.gadbf.org

State Insurance Regulators
Insurance and Fire Safety
Two Martin Luther King, Jr.

Dr.
Atlanta, GA 30334
404–656–2070
Toll free in GA: 1–800–656–2298
TDD/TTY: 404–656–4031
Fax: 404–657–8542
www.inscomm.state.ga.us

State Securities Administrators
Division of Securities and Business Regulation
Office of the Secretary of State
802 West Tower
Two Martin Luther King, Jr. Dr.
Atlanta, GA 30334
404–656–3920
Toll free: 1–888–733–7427
Fax: 404–657–8410
Email:
securities@sos.state.ga.us
www.sos.state.ga.us

State Utility Commissions
Public Service Commission
244 Washington Street
Atlanta, GA 30334
404–656–4501
Toll free in GA: 1–800–282–5813
Fax: (404)656–2341
Email: gapsc@psc.state.ga.us
www.psc.state.ga.us

Hawaii

Office of Consumer Protection
Department of Commerce and Consumer Affairs
345 Kekuanaoa St.
Room 12
Hilo, HI 96720
808–933–0910
Fax: 808–933–8845

Office of Consumer Protection
Department of Commerce and Consumer Affairs
235 South Beretania St.
Room 801
Honolulu, HI 96813–2419
808–586–2636
Fax: 808–586–2640

Office of Consumer Protection
Dept of Commerce and Consumer Affairs
1063 Lower Main St.
Ste C–216
Wailuku, HI 96793
808–984–8244
Fax: 808–243–5807
www.hawaii.gov/dcca/ocp

State Banking Authorities
Division of Financial Institutions
Department of Commerce and Consumer Affairs
335 Merchant Street, Room 221
P.O. Box 2054

Honolulu, HI 96805
808–586–2820
Toll free in Molokai/Lanai: 1–800–468–4644
Toll free in Kauai: 1–800–274–3141
Toll free in Maui: 1–800–984–2400
Toll free in Hawaii: 1–800–974–4000
TDD/TTY: 808–586–2820
Fax: 808–586–2818
Email: dfi@dcca.hawaii.gov
www.hawaii.gov/dcca/dfi

State Insurance Regulators
Insurance Division
Department of Commerce and
Consumer Affairs
P.O. Box 3614
Honolulu, HI 96811–3614
808–586–2790 or 2799
Fax: 808–586–2806
Email:
insurance@dcca.hawaii.gov
www.hawaii.gov/dcca/ins

State Securities Administrators
Business Registration Division
Department of Commerce and
Consumer Affairs
335 Merchant St. Room 204
2nd Floor
Honolulu, HI 96818
808–586–2744
Fax: 808–586–2733

Email:
ryan.s.ushijima@dcca.hawaii.gov
www.hawaii.gov

State Utility Commissions
Public Utilities Commission
465 South King St., Room 103
Honolulu, HI 96813
808–586–2020
Fax: 808–586–2066
Email:
Hawaii.PUC@hawaii.gov
www.hawaii.gov/budget/puc/

Idaho
Consumer Protection Unit
Idaho Attorney General's
Office
650 West State St.
Boise, ID 83720–0010
208–334–2424
Toll free in ID: 1–800–432–3545
Fax: 208–334–2830
www.state.id.us/ag

State Banking Authorities
Department of Finance
PO Box 83720
Boise, ID 83720–0031
208–332–8000
Toll free in ID: 1–888–346–3378
Fax: 208–332–8098
Email: finance@fin.state.id.us
finance.state.id.us/home.asp

State Insurance Regulators

Department of Insurance
700 West State St.
P.O. Box 83720
Boise, ID 83720–0043
208–334–4250
Toll free in ID: 1–800–721–3272
Fax: 208–334–4398
www.doi.state.id.us

State Securities Administrators

Department of Finance
700 W. State St.
2nd Floor
PO Box 83720 (zip 83720–0031)
Boise, ID 83702
208–332–8000
Toll free in ID: 1–888–346–3378
Fax: 208–332–8097
finance.state.id.us/home.asp

State Utility Commissions

Public Utilities Commission
PO Box 83720
Boise, ID 83720–0074
208–334–0300
Toll free in ID: 1–800–432–0369
Voice/TDD Toll free: 1–800–337–1363
TDD: 1–800–377–3529

Fax: 208–334–3762
www.puc.state.id.us

Illinois

Consumer Fraud Bureau
Office of the Attorney General
500 South Second St.
Springfield, IL 62706
217–782–1090
Toll free in IL: 1–800–243–0618
TTY: 217–785–2771 or toll free in IL: 1–877–844–5461
Fax: 217–782–1097
Email:
ag_consumer@atg.state.il.us
www.illinoisattorneygeneral.gov

Consumer Fraud Bureau
1001 East Main St.
Carbondale, IL 62901
618–529–6400
Toll free in IL: 1–800–243–0607
TTY: 618–529–0607 or toll free in IL: 1–877–675–9339
Fax: 618–529–6416
Email:
ag_consumer@atg.state.il.us
www.illinoisattorneygeneral.gov

Consumer Fraud Bureau
100 West Randolph, 12th Floor
Chicago, IL 60601
312–814–3580
Toll free in IL: 1–800–386–5438

TDD: 312–814–3374
Fax: 312–814–2549
Email:
ag_consumer@atg.state.il.us
www.illinoisattorneygeneral.
gov

Governor's Office of Citizens
Assistance
222 South College, Room 106
Springfield, IL 62706
217–782–0244
Toll free in IL: 1–800–642–3112
Fax: 217–524–4049
Email: governor@state.il.us

State Banking Authorities
Division of Banks and Real
Estate
310 South Michigan Ave.
Suite 2130
Chicago, IL 60604
312–793–3000
Toll free: 1–877–793–3470
TDD: 312–793–0291
Fax: 312–793–7097
www.obre.state.il.us

State Insurance Regulators
Division of Insurance
Department of Financial and
Professional Regulation
100 West Randolph St.
Suite 5–570
Chicago, IL 60601-3395
312–814–2420
TDD: 312/814–2603

Fax: 312–14–5435
Email: Director@ins.state.il.us
www.state.il.us/ins

Division of Insurance
Department of Financial and
Professional Regulation
320 West Washington St.
Springfield, IL 62767
217–782–4515
Toll free: 1–877–527–9431
(Office of Consumer Health
Insurance)
TDD: 217–524–4872
Fax: 217–782–5020
Email: director@ins.state.il.us
www.idfpr.com

**State Securities
Administrators**
Securities Department
Secretary of State
300 W. Jefferson St, Suite
300A
Springfield, IL 62702
217–782–2256
217–524–0652
Toll free in IL: 1–800–628–7937
www.sos.state.il.us

State Utility Commissions
Commerce Commission
527 East Capitol Ave.
P.O. Box 19280
Springfield, IL 62794–9280
217–782–7295
Toll free in IL: 1–800–524–0795

TTY toll free: 1–800–858–9277
Fax: 217–524–6859
www.icc.state.il.us

Indiana
Consumer Protection Division
Office of the Attorney General
Indiana Government Center
South
402 West Washington St., 5th
Floor
Indianapolis, IN 46204
317–232–6201
Toll free in IN: 1–800–382–
5516 Consumer Hotline
Fax: 317–232–7979
www.in.gov/attorneygeneral

State Banking Authorities
Department of Financial
Institutions
30 S. Meridian Street, Suite
300
Indianapolis, IN 46204
317–232–3955
Toll free in IN: 1–800–382–
4880
Fax: 317–232–7655
www.in.gov/dfi

State Insurance Regulators
Department of Insurance
311 W. Washington St., Suite
300
Indianapolis, IN 46204–2787
317–232–2385
Toll free in IN: 1–800–622–
4461
Toll free: 1–800–452–4800 (in-
state senior health insurance
information)
Fax: 317–232–5251
www.state.in.us/idoi/

State Securities Administrators
Securities Division
Office of the Secretary of State
302 West Washington
Room E–111
Indianapolis, IN 46204
317–232–6681
Toll free in IN: 1–800–223–
8791
Fax: 317–233–3675
www.state.in.us/sos

State Utility Commissions
Utility Regulatory
Commission
Consumer Affairs Division
302 West Washington St.
Suite E–306
Indianapolis, IN 46204
317–232–2712
Toll free in IN: 1–800–851–
4268
TDD: 317–232–8556
Fax: 317–233–2410
Email:
jjohnson@urc.state.in.us
www.IN.gov/iurc

Iowa

Consumer Protection Division
Office of the Attorney General
1305 East Walnut St.
2nd Floor
Des Moines, IA 50319
515–281–5926
Toll free in IA: 1–888–777–4590
Fax: 515–281–6771
Email:
consumer@ag.state.ia.us
www.IowaAttorneyGeneral.org

State Banking Authorities
Division of Banking
200 East Grand, Suite 300
Des Moines, IA 50309–1827
515–281–4014
Toll free: 1–800–972–2018
Fax: 515–281–4862
Email: idob@max.state.ia.us
www.idob.state.ia.us

State Insurance Regulators
Division of Insurance
330 Maple St.
Des Moines, IA 50319
515–281–5705
Fax: 515–281–3059
www.iid.state.ia.us

State Securities Administrators
Enforcement Section
Securities Bureau
340 Maple St.

Des Moines, IA 50319–0066
515–281–4441
Toll free: 1–800–351–4665
Fax: 515–281–3059
Email: iowasec@iid.state.ia.us
www.iid.state.ia.us/division/securities/default.asp

State Utility Commissions
Utilities Board
350 Maple St.
Des Moines, IA 50319–0069
515–281–3839
Toll free in IA: 1–877–565–4450
Fax: 515–281–5329
Email:
iubcustomer@iub.state.ia.us
www.state.ia.us/iub

Kansas
Consumer Protection & Antitrust Division
Office of the Attorney General
120 SW 10th
2nd Floor
Topeka, KS 66612–1597
785–296–3751
Toll free in KS: 1–800–432–2310
TDD/TTY toll free: 785–291–3767
Fax: 785–291–3699
Email: cprotect@ksag.org
www.ink.org/public/ksag

State Banking Authorities

Office of the State Bank
Commissioner
700 Jackson St., Suite 300
Topeka, KS 66603–3714
785–296–2266
Toll free: 1–877–387–8523
(Consumer Helpline)
Fax: 785–296–0168
www.osbckansas.org

State Insurance Regulators

Insurance Division
420 SW 9th St.
Topeka, KS 66612–1678
785–296–7801
Toll free in KS: 1–800–432–
2484
TDD/TTY toll free 1–877–235–
3151
Fax: 785–296–2283
Email:
commissione4r@ksinsurance.o
rg
www.ksinsurance.org

State Securities Administrators

Office of the Securities
Commissioner
618 South Kansas Ave.
2nd Floor
Topeka, KS 66603–3804
785–296–3307
Toll free in KS: 1–800–232–
9580
Fax: 785–296–6872
Email:

ksecom@cjnetworks.com
www.ink.org/public/ksecom

State Utility Commissions

Corporation Commission
1500 SW Arrowhead Rd.
Topeka, KS 66604–4027
785–271–3100
Toll free in KS: 1–800–662–
0027
TDD toll free 1–800–766–3777
Fax: 785–271—3354
Email:
public.affairs@kcc.state.ks.us
www.kcc.state.ks.us

Kentucky

Consumer Protection Division
Office of the Attorney General
1024 Capital Center Dr.
Frankfort, KY 40601
502–696–5389
Toll free in KY: 1–888–432–
9257
Fax: 502–573–8317
Email:
consumerprotection@ag.ky.go
v
ag.ky.gov

Consumer Protection Division
Office of the Attorney General
8911 Shelbyville Rd.
Louisville, KY 40222
502–425–4825
Fax: 502–573–8317

State Banking Authorities
Department of Financial
Institutions
1025 Capitol Center Dr., Suite
200
Frankfort, KY 40601
502–573–3390
Toll free: 1–800–223–2579
Fax: 502–573–8787
www.dfi.state.ky.us

State Insurance Regulators
Office of Insurance
215 West Main St.
Frankfort, KY 40601
502–564–3630
Toll free: 1–800–595–6053
Fax: 502–564–1650
doi.ppr.ky.gov

**State Securities
Administrators**
Division of Securities
Department of Financial
Institutions
1025 Capitol Center Dr.
Suite. 200
Frankfort, KY 40601–3868
502–573–3390
Toll free: 1–800–223–2579
Fax: 502–573–8787
www.dfi.state.ky.us

State Utility Commissions
Public Service Commission
211 Sower Blvd.
P.O. Box 615

Frankfort, KY 40602
502–564–3940
Toll free in KY: 1–800–772–
4636 (complaints only)
TDD/TTY toll free: 1–800–
648–6056
Fax: 502–564–3460
www.psc.state.ky.us

Louisiana
Consumer Protection Section
Office of the Attorney General
P.O. Box 94005
Baton Rouge, LA 70804–9005
Toll free: 1–800–351–4889
Fax: 225–342–326–6499
www.ag.state.la.us

State Banking Authorities
Office of Financial Institutions
PO Box 94095
Baton Rouge, LA 70804–9095
225–925–4660
Fax: 225–925–4524
Email:
la_ofi@mail.premier.net
www.ofi.state.la.us

State Insurance Regulators
Department of Insurance
1702 N. Third St.
Baton Rouge, LA 70802
225–342–0895/225–342–5900
Toll free: 1–800–259–5300
Toll free: 1–800–259–5301

Fax: 254–342–3078
www.ldi.state.la.us

**State Securities
Administrators**
Securities Division
Office of Financial Institutions
8660 United Plaza Blvd.
2nd Floor
Post Office Box 94095
Baton Rouge, LA 70804–9095
225–925–4660
Fax: 225–925–4548
www.ofi.state.la.us

State Utility Commissions
Public Service Commission
PO Box 91154
Baton Rouge, LA 70821–9154
225–342–4999
Toll free in LA: 1–800–256–
2397
Fax: 225–342–2831
www.lpsc.org

Maine
Consumer Protection Division
Office of the Attorney General
6 State Home Station
Augusta, ME 04333
207–626–8800
Fax: 207–626–8812
Email:
consumer.mediation@state.me
.us
www.maine.gov

Office of Consumer Credit
Regulation
35 State Home Station
Augusta, ME 04333–0035
207–624–8527
Toll free in ME: 1–800–332–
8529
TDD/TTY: 207–624–8563
Fax: 207–582–7699
www.mainecreditreg.org

State Banking Authorities
Bureau of Financial
Institutions
36 State Home Station
Augusta, ME 04333–0036
207–624–8570
Toll free: 1–800–965–5235
TDD: 207–624–8563
Fax: 207–624–8590
www.mainebankingreg.org

State Insurance Regulators
Bureau of Insurance
34 State Home Station
Augusta, ME 04333
207–624–8475
Toll free in ME: 1–800–300–
5000
TDD: 207–624–8563
Fax: 207–624–8599
www.maineinsurancereg.org

**State Securities
Administrators**
Office of Securities
121 State Home Station

Augusta, ME 04333–0018
207–624–8551
Toll free in ME: 1–800–624–8551
TDD/TTY: 207–624–8563
Fax: 207–624–8590
www.mainesecuritiesreg.org

State Utility Commissions
Public Utilities Commission
242 State St.
Augusta, ME 04333–0018
207–287–3831
Toll free in ME: 1–800–452–4699
TTY toll free: 1–800–437–1220
Fax: 207–287–1039
Email: maine.puc@maine.gov
www.state.me.us/mpuc/

Maryland
Consumer Protection Division
Office of the Attorney General
200 Saint Paul Place
16th Floor
Baltimore, MD 21202–2021
410–528–8662 (Consumer Complaints)
410–576–6550 (Consumer Information)
410–528–1840 (Health Advocacy unit)
TDD: 410–576–6372 (Maryland only)
Fax: 410–576–7040
Email: consumer@oag.state.md.us

www.oag.state.md.us/consumer

Regional Offices
Consumer Protection Division
Maryland Attorney Generals' Office
138 East Antietam St., Ste. 210
Hagerstown, MD 21740–5684
301–791–4780
TDD/TTY: 410–576–6372
Fax: 301–791–7178

Consumer Protection Division
Eastern Shore Branch Office
Office of the Attorney General
201 Baptist St.
Suite 30
Salisbury, MD 21801–4976
410–543–6620
Fax: 410–543–6642
www.oag.state.md.us

State Banking Authorities
Commissioner of Financial Regulation
500 North Calvert St.
Suite 402
Baltimore, MD 21202
410–230–6100
Toll free in MD: 1–888–784–0136
TTY: 410–767–2117
Fax: 410–333–0475
Email: fin_reg@dllr.state.md.us
www.dllr.state.md.us/finance

State Insurance Regulators
Insurance Administration
525 St. Paul Place
Baltimore, MD 212022272
410–468–2000
Toll free: 1–800–492–6116
TTY toll free: 1–800–735–2258
Fax: 410–468–2020
www.mdinsurance.state.md.us

State Securities Administrators
Securities Division
Office of the Attorney General
200 Saint Paul Place
Baltimore, MD 21202–
410–576–6360
Toll free: 888–743–0023
TDD: 410–576–6372
Email: securities@oag.state.md.us
www.oag.state.md.us/Securities/

State Utility Commissions
Public Service Commission
6 St. Paul St.
16th Floor
Baltimore, MD 21202–6806
410–767–8000
Toll free in MD: 1–800–492–0474
TDD toll free in MD: 1–800–735–2258
Fax: 410–333–6495

Email: mpsc@psc.state.md.us
www.psc.state.md.us/psc/

Massachusetts
Executive Office of Consumer Affairs and Business Regulation
10 Park Plaza
Room 5170
Boston, MA 02116
617–973–8700 (General Information)
617–973–8787 (Consumer Hotline)
Toll free in MA: 1–888–283–3757
TDD/TTY: 617–973–8790
Fax: 617–973–8798
Email: consumer@state.ma.us
www.mass.gov/Consumer

Consumer Protection and Antitrust Division
Office of the Attorney General
One Ashburton Place
Boston, MA 02108
617–727–8400 (Consumer Hotline)
Fax: 617–727–3265
www.mass.gov/ago

Southern Massachusetts Division
Office of the Attorney General
105 William Street
New Bedford, MA 02740

163

508–990–9700
Fax: 508–990–8686
Western Massachusetts
Division
Office of the Attorney General
436 Dwight St.
Springfield, MA 01103
413–784–1240
Fax: 413–784–1244
www.ago.state.ma.us

Central Massachusetts
Division
Office of the Attorney General
One Exchange Place
Worcester, MA 01608
508–792–7600
Fax: 508–795–1991

State Banking Authorities
Division of Banks
One South Station
Boston, MA 02110
617–956–1500
Toll free in MA: 1–800–495–2265
TDD: 617–956–1577
Fax: 617–956–1597
www.mass.gov/dob

State Insurance Regulators
Division of Insurance
Consumer Service Section
One South Station, 5th Floor
Boston, MA 02110
617–521–7777
TDD: 617–521–7490

Fax: 617–521–7575
www.state.ma.us/doi

State Securities Administrators
Office of the Secretary of State
One Ashburton Place
Room 1701
Boston, MA 02108
617–727–3548
Toll free in MA: 1–800–269–5428
TDD/TTY: 617–878–3889
Fax: 617–248–0177
Email:
securities@sec.state.ma.us
www.sec.state.ma.us/sct

State Utility Commissions
Dept. of Telecommunications
and Energy
1 South Station
12th Floor
Boston, MA 02110
617–305–3500
Toll free: 1–800–392–6066
TDD toll free: 1–800–323–6066
Fax: 617–478–2591
www.magnet.state.ma.us/dpu

Michigan
Consumer Protection Division
Office of Attorney General
PO Box 30213
Lansing, MI 48909
517–373–1140

Toll free: 1–877–765–8388
Fax: 517–241–3771

State Banking Authorities
Office of Financial and
Insurance Services
611 W. Ottawa St.
3rd Floor
P.O. Box 30220
Lansing, MI 489330220
517–373–3460
Toll free: 1–877–999–6442
Fax: 517–335–4978
www.michigan.gov/ofis

State Insurance Regulators
Office of Financial and
Insurance Services
611 West Ottawa St., 3rd Floor
P.O. Box 30220
Lansing, MI 48933
517–373–0220
Toll free: 1–877–999–6442
Fax: 517–335–4978
www.michigan.gov/ofis

**State Securities
Administrators**
Office of Financial and
Insurance Services
611 W. Ottawa St.
3rd Floor
P.O. Box 30220
Lansing, MI 48909
517–373–0220
Toll Free: 1–877–999–6442

Fax: 517–335–4978
www.michigan.gov/ofis

State Utility Commissions
Public Service Commission
6545 Mercantile Way
Suite 7
P.O. Box 30221
Lansing, MI 48909
517–241–6180
Toll free in MI: 1–800–292–
9555
Fax: 517–241–6181
Email:
mpsc_commissioners@michig
an.gov
www.michigan.gov/mpsc

Minnesota
Consumer Services Division
Attorney General's Office
1400 NCL Tower
445 Minnesota St.
St. Paul, MN 55101
612–296–3353
Toll free: 1–800–657–3787
Fax: 612–282–2155
Email:
attorney.general@state.mn.us
www.ag.state.mn.us/consume
r

State Banking Authorities
Financial Examinations
Division
Department of Commerce

85 Seventh Place East, Suite 500
St. Paul, MN 55101
651–296–2715
Fax: 651–296–8591
Email:
kevin.murphy@state.mn.us
www.commerce.state.mn.us

State Insurance Regulators
Department of Commerce
Market Assurance Division
85 7th Place East
St. Paul, MN 55101
651–296–2488
Toll free in MN: 1–800–657–3602
Fax: 651–296–4328
Email:
insurance.commerce@state.mn.us
www.commerce.state.mn.us

State Securities Administrators
Department of Commerce
85 Seventh Place East
Suite 500
St. Paul, MN 55101
651–296–4026
Toll free in MN: 1–800–657–3602
TDD: 651–296–2860
Fax: 651–296–4328
Email:
securities.commerce@state.mn.us
www.commerce.state.mn.us

State Utility Commissions
Public Utilities Commission
121 7th Place East
Suite 350
St. Paul, MN 55101–2147
651–296–0406
Toll free: 1–800–657–3782
TDD: 651–297–1200
Fax: 651–297–7073
Email:
consumer.puc@state.mn.us
www.puc.state.mn.us

Mississippi
Bureau of Regulatory Services
Department of Agriculture and Commerce
121 North Jefferson St.
P.O. Box 1609
Jackson, MS 39201
601–359–1111
Fax: 601–359–1175
www.mdac.state.ms.us

Consumer Protection Division
Attorney General's Office
P.O. Box 22947
Jackson, MS 39225–2947
601–359–4230
Toll free in MS: 1–800–281–4418
Fax: 601–359–4231
www.ago.state.ms.us

State Banking Authorities
Department of Banking and
Consumer Finance
P.O. Box 23729
Jackson, MS 39205–3729
601–359–1031
Toll free in MS: 1–800–844–2499
Fax: 601–359–3557
Email: bass@dbcf.state.ms.us
www.dbcf.state.ms.us

State Insurance Regulators
Department of Insurance
PO Box 79
Jackson, MS 39205
601–359–3569
Toll free in MS: 1–800–562–2957
Fax: 601–359–1077
Email:
consumer@mid.state.ms.us
www.doi.state.ms.us

**State Securities
Administrators**
Business Regulation and
Enforcement
Secretary of State's Office
700 North St.
or P.O. Box 136 (Zip 39205–0136)
Jackson, MS 39202
601–359–1350
Toll free: 1–800–256–3494
Fax: 601–359–1499

Email: jnelson@sos.state.ms.us
www.sos.state.ms.us

State Utility Commissions
Public Service Commission
Woolfolk Building
501 N West St.
Jackson, MS 39201
(601) 961–5440 (Southern
District)
(601) 961–5430 (Central
District)
(601) 961–5450 (Chairman &
Northern District)
Toll–free: (800) 356–6429
(Southern District)
Toll–free: 1–800–356–6430
(Central District)
Toll free: (800) 637–7722
(Chairman & Northern
District)
Fax: 601–961–5464 (Chairman
& Northern District)
www.psc.state.ms.us

Missouri
Consumer Protection and
Trade Offense Division
PO Box 899
1530 Rax Court
Jefferson City, MO 65102
573–751–6887
573–751–3321
Toll free in MO: 1–800–392–8222
TDD/TTY toll free in MO: 1–800–729–8668

Fax: 573–751–7948
Email: attgenmail@moago.org
www.ago.state.mo.us

State Banking Authorities
Department of Finance
PO Box 716
Jefferson City, MO 65102
573–751–3242
Fax: 573–751–9192
Email: finance@ded.mo.gov
www.missouri–finance.org

State Insurance Regulators
Missouri Department of
Insurance
PO Box 690
301 West High St., Room 530
Jefferson City, MO 651020690
573–751–4126
Toll free in MO: 1–800–726–
7390
TDD/TTY: 573–526–4536
Fax: 573–751–1165
www.insurance.state.mo.us

**State Securities
Administrators**
Commissioner of Securities
PO Box 1276
Jefferson City, MO 65102
573–751–4136
Toll free in MO: 1–800–721–
7996
Fax: 573–526–3124
ago.missouri.gov/divisions/co
nsumerprotection.htm

State Utility Commissions
Public Service Commission
PO Box 360
Jefferson City, MO 65102
573–751–3234
Toll free in MO: 1–800–392–
4211
TDD toll free in MO: 711
Fax: 573–526–1500
www.psc.mo.gov

Montana
Montana Office of Consumer
Protection
Department of Justice
1219 8th Ave.
PO Box 200151
Helena, MT 59620–0151
406–444–4500
Fax: 406–444–9680
doj.mt.gov/consumer

State Banking Authorities
Division of Banking &
Financial Institutions
301 South Park
Suite 316
PO Box 200546
Helena, MT 59620–0546
406–841–2920
Fax: 406–841–2930
www.discoveringmontana.co
m/doa/banking

State Insurance Regulators
Department of Insurance
840 Helena Ave.

Helena, MT 59601
406–444–2040
Toll free in MT: 1–800–332–6148
Fax: 406–444–3497
www.state.mt.us/sao

State Securities Administrators
Securities Division
State Auditor
840 Helena Ave.
Helena, MT 59601
406–444–2040
Toll free in MT: 1–800–332–6148
Fax: 406–444–3497
www.sao.state.mt.us

State Utility Commissions
Public Service Commission
1701 Prospect Ave.
P.O. Box 202601
Helena, MT 59620–2601
406–444–6199
Toll free in MT: 1–800–646–6150
TDD: 406–444–6199
Fax: 406–444–7618
www.psc.state.mt.us

Nebraska
Office of the Attorney General
Department of Justice
2115 State Capitol
P.O. Box 98920
Lincoln, NE 68509

402–471–2682
402–471–3891 (Spanish)
Toll free in NE: 1–800–727–6432
Toll free in NE: 1–800–850–7555 (Spanish)
Fax: 402–471–0006
www.nol.org/home/ago

State Banking Authorities
Department of Banking & Finance
1230 "O" St., Suite 400
PO Box 95006
Lincoln, NE 68509–5006
402–471–2171
Fax: 402–471–3062
www.ndbf.org

State Insurance Regulators
Department of Insurance
Terminal Building
941 "O" St., Suite 400
Lincoln, NE 685083639
402–471–2201
Toll free in NE: 1–877–564–7323
TDD toll free: 1–800–833–7351
Fax: Fax: 402–471–6559
www.nol.org/home/NDOI

State Securities Administrators
Department of Banking & Finance
Bureau of Securities
PO Box 95006

The Atrium, 1200 N St., Suite
311
Lincoln, NE 68509–5006
402–471–3445
www.ndbf.org

State Utility Commissions
Public Service Commission
300 The Atrium, 1200 N St.
P.O. Box 94927 (68508–4927)
Lincoln, NE 68509
402–471–3101
Toll free in NB: 1–800–526–
0017
TDD: 402–471–0213
Fax: 402–471–0254
Email: celton@mail.state.ne.us
www.psc.state.ne.us

Nevada
Consumer Protection Agency
Bureau of Consumer
Protection
555 E. Washington Ave.
Suite 3900
Las Vegas, NV 89101
702–486–3420
Consumer Affairs Division
1850 East Sahara Ave
Suite 101
Las Vegas, NV 89104
702–486–7355
Toll free: 1–800–326–5202
TDD: 702–486–7901/Fax: 702–
486–7371
Email: ncad@fyiconsumer.org
www.fyiconsumer.org

Consumer Affairs Division
4600 Kietzke Lane, Building B,
Suite 113
Reno, NV 89502
775–688–1800
Toll free in NV: 1–800–326–
5202
TDD: 702–486–7901
Fax: 775–688–1803
Email:
renocad@fyiconsumer.org
www.fyiconsumer.org

State Banking Authorities
Financial Institutions Division
Department of Business &
Industry
2501 E. Sahara Ave, #300
Las Vegas, NV 89704
702–486–4120
Fax: 702–486–4563
Email: ctidd@fid.state.nv.us
www.fid.state.nv.us

State Insurance Regulators
Division of Insurance
Department of Business &
Industry
788 Fairview Drive, Suite 300
Carson City, NV 89701
775–687–7650
Fax: Fax: 775–687–3937
Email: insinfo@doi.state.nv.us
www.doi.state.nv.us/

Division of Insurance
Department of Business &

Industry
2501 East Sahara Ave, Suite
302
Las Vegas, NV 89104
(702) 486–4009
Fax: Fax: 702–486–4007
www.doi.state.nv.us/

**State Securities
Administrators**
Securities Division
Office of the Secretary of State
555 East Washington Ave.
Suite 5200
Las Vegas, NV 89101
702–486–2440
Fax: 702–486–2452
Email: nvsec@sos.nv.gov
www.sos.state.nv.us

State Utility Commissions
Public Utilities Commission
1150 East William St.
Carson City, NV 89701
775–687–6001
702–486–2600 (Las Vegas)
775–738–4914 (Elko)
Toll free in NV: 1–800–992–
0900 ext 87–6001
Fax: 775–687–6110
www.puc.state.nv.us

New Hampshire
Consumer Protection and
Antitrust Bureau
Attorney General's Office
33 Capitol St.

Concord, NH 03301
603–271–3641
TDD toll free: 1–800–735–2964
Fax: 603–271–2110
www.doj.nh.gov/consumer/in
dex.html

State Banking Authorities
State Banking Department
64B Old Suncook Rd.
Concord, NH 03301
603–271–3561
TDD/TTY toll free: 1–800–
735–2964
Fax: 603–271–1090
www.state.nh.us/banking

State Insurance Regulators
Department of Insurance
21 South Fruit St., Suite 14
Concord, NH 03301–2430
603–271–2261
Toll free in NH: 1–800–852–
3416
TDD/TTY toll free in NH: 1–
800–735–2964
Fax: 603–271–0248
Email:
requests@ins.state.nh.us
www.nh.gov/insurance

**State Securities
Administrators**
Bureau of Securities
Regulation
Department of State
State Home

Room 204
Concord, NH 03301–4989
603–271–1463
Fax: 603–271–7933
www.sos.nh.gov/securities

State Utility Commissions
Public Utilities Commission
21 South Fruit St, Suite 10
Bldg. No. 1
Concord, NH 03301–2429
603–271–2431
TDD toll free in NH: 1–800–735–2964
Fax: 603–271–3878
Email: www.puc.nh.gov
www.puc.state.nh.us

New Jersey
Division of Consumer Affairs
Department of Law and
Public Safety
124 Halsey St
PO Box 45025
Newark, NJ 07102
973–504–6200
Toll free in NJ: 1–800–242–5846
Email:
askconsumeraffairs@lps.state.nj.us
www.state.nj.us/lps/ca/home.htm

County Offices
Atlantic County Division of
Consumer Affairs

1333 Atlantic Ave., 8th Floor
Atlantic City, NJ 08401
609–343–2376/609–345–6700
Fax: 609–343–2322

Camden County Office of
Consumer Protection/Weights
and Measures
DiPiero Center
Lakeland Rd.
Blackwood, NJ 08012
856–374–6161 (Consumer
Protection)
856–374–6001 (Weights &
Measures)
Toll free in NJ: 1–800–999–9045
Fax: 856–232–0748
www.camdencounty.com

Cumberland County
Department of Consumer
Affairs/Weight & Measures
788 East Commerce St.
Bridgeton, NJ 08302
856–453–2203
Fax: 856–453–2206
Email:
louismo@co.cumberland.nj.us

Cape May County Consumer
Affairs Weights and Measures
4 Moore Rd. DN 310\302
Cape May Court Home, NJ
08210
609–463–6475
Fax: 609–463–6472

Email: mbrogan@co.cape–
may.nj.us
www.capemaycountygov.net

Essex County Division of
Community
Action/Consumer Services
50 South Clinton St., Suite
3201
East Orange, NJ 07018
973–395–8350
Fax: 973–395–8433

Hunterdon County Office of
Consumer Affairs
PO Box 2900
Flemington, NJ 08822
908–806–5174
Fax: 908–806–2057
Email:
jferrari@co.hunterdon.nj.us

Monmouth County
Department of Consumer
Affairs
50 East Main St.
P.O. Box 1255
Freehold, NJ 07728–1255
732–431–7900
Fax: 732–845–2037

Bergen County Office of
Consumer Protection
One Bergen County Plaza, 3rd
Floor
Hackensack, NJ 07601–7000

201–336–6400
Fax: 201–336–6414

Hudson County Division of
Consumer Affairs
583 Newark Ave.
Jersey City, NJ 07306
201–795–6295/201–795–6163
Fax: 201–795–6468

Burlington County Office of
Consumer Affairs/Weights
and Measures
49 Rancocas Rd.
P.O. Box 6000
Mount Holly, NJ 08060
609–265–5098 (Weights &
Measures)
609–265–5054 (Consumer
Affairs)
Fax: 609–265–5065

Middlesex County Consumer
Affairs
Middlesex County
Administration Building
JFK Square, 2nd Floor, Suite
290
New Brunswick, NJ 08901
732–745–3875
Fax: 732–745–3815
www.co.midddlesex.nj.us

Somerset County Division of
Consumer Affairs
PO Box 3000

Somerville, NJ 08876–1262
908–203–6080
Fax: 908–575–3905
Email:
consumeraffairs@co.somerset.
nj.us
www.co.somerset.nj.us

Ocean County Department of
Consumer Affairs/Weights
and Measures
1027 Hooper Ave.
PO Box 2191
Toms River, NJ 08754–2191
732–929–2105
Toll free in NJ: 1–800–722–
0291 ex. 2105
Fax: 732–506–5330

Mercer County Consumer
Affairs
640 South Broad St., Rm 404
P.O. Box 8068
Trenton, NJ 08650–0068
609–989–6671
Fax: 609–989–6670

Passaic County Department of
Consumer Protection/Weights
and Measures
Dept of Law
1310 Route 23 North
Wayne, NJ 07470
973–305–5750 (Weights &
Measures)
973–305–5881 (Consumer
Protection)

Fax: 973–628–1796
Email:
barbaram@passaiccountynj.or
g

Union County Division of
Consumer Affairs
300 North Ave. East
Westfield, NJ 07090
908–654–9840
Fax: 908–654–3082
Email: fpeterson@ucnj.org
www.unioncountynj.org

Gloucester County
Department of Consumer
Protection
Weights and Measures
115 Budd Blvd.
Woodbury, NJ 08096
856–384–6855
TDD: 856–848–6616
Fax: 856–384–6858
Email:
hspence@co.gloucester.nj.us
co.gloucester.nj.us/protection

State Banking Authorities
Department of Banking and
Insurance
20 West State St.
P.O. Box 325
Trenton, NJ 08625
609–292–3420 (Banking)
Fax: 609–292–5571
www.njdobi.org/

State Insurance Regulators
Department of Banking and
Insurance
20 West State St.
P.O. Box 325
Trenton, NJ 08625
609–633–7667
Fax: 609–292–5571
www.njdobi.org

**State Securities
Administrators**
Bureau of Securities
Department of Law and
Public Safety
PO Box 47029 (07101)
153 Halsey St.
6th Floor
Newark, NJ 07102
973–504–3600
Fax: 973–504–3601
www.state.nj.us/lps/ca/home.
htm

State Utility Commissions
Board of Public Utilities
Two Gateway Center
Newark, NJ 07102
Toll free in NJ: 1–800–624–
0241
www.bpu.state.nj.us

New Mexico
Consumer Protection Division
PO Drawer 1508
407 Galisteo

Santa Fe, NM 87504–1508
505–827–6060
Toll free in NM: 1–800–678–
1508
Fax: 505–827–6685
www.ago.state.nm.us

State Banking Authorities
Financial Institutions Division
Regulation and Licensing
Department
2550 Cerrillos Rd.
3rd Floor
Santa Fe, NM 87501
505–426–4885
Fax: 505–476–4670
Email: rldfid@state.nm.us
www.rld.state.nm.us/FID/

State Insurance Regulators
Department of Insurance
P.O. Box 1269
Santa Fe, NM 87504–1269
505–827–4601
Toll free in NM: 1–800–947–
4722
Fax: 505–827–4734
www.nmprc.state.nm.us

**State Securities
Administrators**
Securities Division
Regulation & Licensing
Department
2550 Cerrillos Road
Santa Fe, NM 87505

505–476–4580
Toll free in NM: 1–800–704–5533
Fax: 505–984–0617
www.rld.state.nm.us

State Utility Commissions
Public Regulation
Commission
Consumer Relations Division
PO Drawer 1269
Santa Fe, NM 87504–1269
505–827–6940
Toll free in NM: 1–800–663–9782
Toll free in NM: 1–800–947–4722
TDD: 505–827–6911
Fax: 505–827–6973
Email:
BarbaraA.Roel@state.nm.us
www.nmprc.state.nm.us/

New York
New York State Consumer
Protection Board
5 Empire State Plaza, Suite 2101
Albany, NY 12223–1556
518–474–8583 (Capitol Region)
Toll free: 1–800–697–1220
Fax: 518–474–2474
Email: webmaster@state.ny.us
www.nysconsumer.gov

Bureau of Consumer Frauds
and Protection
Office of the Attorney General
State Capitol
Albany, NY 12224
518–474–5481
Toll free in NY: 1–800–771–7755
TDD/TTY toll free: 1–800–788–9898
Fax: 518–474–3618
www.oag.state.ny.us

Consumer Frauds and
Protection Bureau
Office of the Attorney General
120 Broadway, 3rd Fl.
New York, NY 10271
212–416–8000
212–416–8345
1–800–771–7755
1–800–788–9898 or 212–416–8893
Fax: 212–416–6003

Regional Offices
Binghamton Regional Office
Office of the Attorney General
State Office Building, 17th
Floor
44 Hawley St.
Binghamton, NY 13901–4433
607–721–8771

Brooklyn Regional Office
Office of the Attorney General
55 Hanson Place, Room 732

Brooklyn, NY 11217
718–722–3949

Buffalo Regional Office
Office of the Attorney General
Statler Towers
107 Delaware Ave.
Buffalo, NY 14202–3473
716–853–8400

Hauppauge Regional Office
Office of the Attorney General
300 Motor Pkwy.
Suite 205
Hauppauge, NY 11788–5127
516–231–2400

Harlem Regional Office
Office of the Attorney General
163 West 125th St.
New York, NY 10027–8201
212–961–4475
Fax: 212–961–4003

Minneola Regional Office
Office of the Attorney General
200 Old Country Rd.
New York, NY 11501
516–248–3302

Plattsburgh Regional Office
Office of Attorney General
70 Clinton St.
Plattsburgh, NY 12901–2818
518–562–3282

Rochester Regional Office
Office of the Attorney General
144 Exchange Blvd., 2nd Floor
Rochester, NY 14614
585–546–7430
TDD: 585–327–3249
Fax: 585–546–7514
Email:
bobby.colon@oag.state.ny.us

Syracuse Regional Office
Office of the Attorney General
615 Erie Blvd. West, Suite 102
Syracuse, NY 13204–2465
315–448–4848
Fax: 315–448–4851

Utica Regional Office
Office of the Attorney General
207 Genesee St., Room 508
Utica, NY 13501
315–793–2225
Fax: 315–793–2228

Watertown Regional Office
Office of the Attorney General
Dulles State Office Building
317 Washington Street
Watertown, NY 13601–3744
315–785–2444

Westchester Regional Office
Office of the Attorney General
101 East Post Rd.
White Plains, NY 10601–5008
914–422–8755
Fax: 914–422–8706

State Banking Authorities
Banking Department
One State Street
New York, NY 10004
212–709–5470
Toll free in NY: 1–877–BANK–
NYS (consumer services
hotline)
Fax: 212–709–3582
www.banking.state.ny.us

State Insurance Regulators
Consumer Services Bureau
Insurance Department
One Commerce Plaza
Albany, NY 12257
518–474–6600
Toll free: 1–800–342–3736
Fax: 518–474–6630
www.ins.state.ny.us

Consumer Services Bureau
Insurance Department
65 Court St. #7
Buffalo, NY 14202
716–847–7618
Toll free in NY: 1–800–342–
3736
Fax: 716–847–7925
www.ins.state.ny.us

**State Securities
Administrators**
Bureau of Investor Protection
and Securities
Office of the Attorney General

120 Broadway
New York, NY 10271
212–416–8200
Fax: 212–416–8816
www.oag.state.ny.us

State Utility Commissions
Public Service Commission
Office of Retail Market
Development
3 Empire State Plaza
Albany, NY 12223–1350
518–474–1540/Toll free in NY:
1–877–342–3377 – Complaints
(complaints – gas, electric,
telephone)
Toll free: 1–888–ASK–PSCI
(275–7721) – PSC Competition
Information
Toll free: 1–866–GRN–PWR
(476–7697) – Green Power
Information
Fax: 518–474–1691
Email:
ronald_cerniglia@dps.state.ny
.us
askpsc.com

North Carolina
Consumer Protection Division
Office of the Attorney General
9001 Mail Service Center
Raleigh, NC 27699–9001
919–716–6400
Toll free in NC: 1–877–566–
7226

Fax: 919–716–6050
www.ncdoj.com

State Banking Authorities
North Carolina Commissioner
of Banks
4309 Mail Service Center
Raleigh, NC 27699–4309
919–733–3016
Fax: 919–733–6918
www.banking.state.nc.us

State Insurance Regulators
Department of Insurance
Dobbs Bldg.
430 North Salisbury St.
1201 Mail Service Center
Raleigh, NC 27699–1201
919–733–7349
Toll free: 1–800–546–5664
Toll free: 1–800–662–7777
Fax: 919–733–0085
Email: consumer@ncdoi.net
www.ncdoi.com

State Securities
Administrators
Securities Division
2 South Salisbury St.
Raleigh, NC 27601
919–733–3924
Toll free: 1–800–688–4507
(investor hotline)
Fax: 919–821–0818
www.sosnc.com

State Utility Commissions

NC Utilities Commission –
Public Staff
Consumer Services
4326 Mail Service Center
Raleigh, NC 27699–4326
919–733–9277
Fax: 919–733–4744
Email:
consumer.services@ncmail.net
www.ncuc.commerce.state.nc.
us/

North Dakota
Consumer Protection and
Antitrust Division
Office of the Attorney General
4205 State Street
PO Box 1054
Bismarck, ND 58502–1054
701–328–3404
Toll free in ND: 1–800–472–
2600
TTY toll free: 1–800–366–6888
Fax: 701–328–5568
Email: cpat@state.nd.us
www.ag.state.nd.us

State Banking Authorities
Department of Financial
Institutions
2000 Schafer St.
Suite G
Bismarck, ND 58501–1204
701–328–9933
TDD toll free in ND: 1–800–
366–6888
Fax: 701–328–9955

Email: dfi@state.nd.us
www.discovernd.com/dfi

State Insurance Regulators
Insurance Department
600 East Boulevard Ave.
5th Floor
Bismarck, ND 58505
701–328–2440
Toll free in ND: 1–800–247–0560
TDD/TTY toll free: 1–800–366–6888
Fax: 701–328–4880
Email: insurance@state.nd.us
www.state.nd.us/ndins

State Securities Administrators
Securities Department
State Capitol – 5th Floor
600 E. Boulevard Ave.
Dept. 414
Bismarck, ND 58505–0510
701–328–2910
Toll free in ND: 1–800–297–5124
Fax: 701–328–2946
Email: ndsecurities@state.nd.us
www.ndsecurities.com

State Utility Commissions
Public Service Commission
600 E. Boulevard Ave., Dept 408
12th Floor

Bismarck, ND 58505–0480
701–328–2400
TDD toll free in ND: 1–800–366–6888
Fax: 701–328–2410
Email: ndpsc@psc.state.nd.us
www.psc.state.nd.us

Ohio
Ohio Consumers' Counsel
10 W. Broad St.
18th Floor
Columbus, OH 43215
614–466–8574 (outside OH)
Toll free in OH: 1–877–742–5622
Email: occ@occ.state.oh.us
wwww.pickoca.org

Consumer Protection Section
Attorney General's Office
30 East Broad St.
14th Floor
Columbus, OH 43215–3428
614–466–8831
Toll free in OH: 1–800–282–0515
TDD: 614–466–1393
Fax: 614–728–7583
Email: consumer@ag.state.oh.us
www.ag.state.oh.us

County Offices
Summit County Office of Consumer Affairs
PO Box 22448

Akron, OH 44302–2448
330–643–2879
Email:
consumeraffairs@summitoh.n
et
www.co.summit.oh.us/conaff
airs.htm

State Banking Authorities
Division of Financial
Institutions
Department of Commerce
77 South High St.
21st Floor
Columbus, OH 43215–6120
614–728–8400
614–466–2932
Fax: 614–644–1631
www.com.state.oh.us/ODOC/
dfi/

State Insurance Regulators
Office of Consumer Services
Department of Insurance
2100 Stella Court
Columbus, OH 43215–1067
614–644–3378
Toll free: 1–800–686–1526
(consumer hotline)
Toll free: 1–800–686–1527
(fraud hotline)
Toll free: 1–800–686–1578
(senior hotline)
TDD/TTY: 614–644–3745
Fax: 614–387–1302
Email:

nancy.colley@ins.state.oh.us
www.ohioinsurance.gov

**State Securities
Administrators**
Division of Securities
77 South High St.
22nd Floor
Columbus, OH 43215
614–644–7381
Toll free: 1–800–788–1194
(investor protection hotline)
Fax: 614–466–3316
www.securities.state.oh.us

State Utility Commissions
Public Utilities Commission
180 East Broad St.
Columbus, OH 43215–3793
614–466–3292
Toll free in OH: 1–800–686–
7826
TDD toll free in OH: 1–800–
686–1570
Fax: 614–752–8351
www.puc.state.oh.us

Oklahoma
Commission on Consumer
Credit
4545 North Lincoln Blvd.,
#104
Oklahoma City, OK 73105
405–521–3653
Toll free: 1–800–448–4904
Fax: 405–521–6740
Email:

dhardin@okdocc.state.ok.us
www.okdocc.state.ok.us

Consumer Protection Unit
Oklahoma Attorney General
4545 N. Lincoln Ave.
Suite 260
Oklahoma City, OK 73105
405–521–2029
Fax: 405–528–1867
www.oag.state.ok.us

State Banking Authorities
State Banking Department
4545 North Lincoln Blvd.
Suite 164
Oklahoma City, OK 73105
405–521–2782
Fax: 405–522–2993
www.osbd.state.ok.us

State Insurance Regulators
Insurance Department
2401 N. W. 23rd St.
Suite 28
PO Box 53408
Oklahoma City, OK 73152–3408
405–521–2828
Toll free in OK: 1–800–522–0071
Fax: 405–521–6635
Email: okinsdpt@telepath.com
www.oid.state.ok.us

State Securities Administrators

Department of Securities
First National Center
120 North Robinson
Suite 860
Oklahoma City, OK 73102
405–280–7700
Fax: 405–280–7742
Email:
general@securities.state.ok.us
www.securities.state.ok.us

State Utility Commissions
Corporation Commission
PO Box 52000
Oklahoma City, OK 73152–2000
405–521–2211/
Toll free in OK: 1–800–522–8154
TDD: 405–521–3513/Fax: 405–521–2087
www.occeweb.com

Oregon
Financial Fraud/Consumer
Protection Section
Department of Justice
1162 Court St., NE
Salem, OR 97310
503–947–4333/503–378–4320
(Hotline Salem only)
503–229–5576 (Hotline
Portland Only)
Toll free in OR: 1–877–877–9392
TDD/TTY: 503–378–5939

Fax: 503–378–5017
www.doj.state.or.us

State Banking Authorities
Department of Consumer &
Business Services – Division
of Finance and Corporate
Securities
350 Winter St., NE, Room 410
Salem, OR 97310
503–378–4140/Toll free: 1–866–
814–9710
(Fraud and complaint
investigation)
TTY: 503–378–4100
Fax: 503–947–7862
Email:
dcbs.dfcsmail@state.or.us
www.oregondfcs.org

State Insurance Regulators
Insurance Division
350 Winter St., NE, Room
440–2
P.O. Box 14480
Salem, OR 97310–3883
503–947–7984
Toll free in OR: 1–888–877–
4894
Fax: 503–378–4351
Email:
dcbs.insmail@state.or.us
insurance.oregon.gov

**State Securities
Administrators**

Department of Consumer &
Business Services
Division of Finance and
Corporate Securities
350 Winter St., NE,
Suite 410
Salem, OR 97310
503–378–4140
Toll free: 1–866–814–9710
TTY: (503) 378–4100
Fax: 503–947–7862
Email:
dcbs.fcsmail@state.or.us
egov.oregon.gov/DCBS

State Utility Commissions
Public Utility Commission
Consumer Services Division
550 Capitol St., NE, Suite 215
PO Box 2148
Salem, OR 97308–2148
503–378–6600
Toll free in OR: 1–800–522–
2404 (consumer services only)
Toll free in OR: 1–800–553–
9600
Fax: 503–378–5743
Email:
puc.consumer@state.or.us
www.puc.state.or.us

Pennsylvania
Office of the Consumer
Advocate
Office of the Attorney General
Forum Place, 5th Floor
Harrisburg, PA 17101–1921

717–783–5048 (Utilities only)
Toll free in PA: 1–800–684–6560
Fax: 717–783–7152
Email: consumer@paoca.org
www.oca.state.pa.us

Bureau of Consumer Protection
Office of Attorney General
14th Floor, Strawberry Square
Harrisburg, PA 17120
717–787–9707
Toll free in PA: 1–800–441–2555
Toll free in PA: 1–877–888–4877 (Health Care Section)
Fax: 717–787–1190
www.attorneygeneral.gov

Regional Offices
Allentown Regional Office –
Bureau of Consumer Protection
Office of Attorney General
801 Hamilton St., 4th Floor
Allentown, PA 18101
610–821–6690
Fax: 610–821–6529

Ebensburg Regional Office –
Bureau of Consumer Protection
Office of Attorney General
171 Lovell Ave., Suite 202
Ebensburg, PA 15931

814–471–1831
Fax: 814–471–1840

Erie Regional Office – Bureau of Consumer Protection
Office of the Attorney General
1001 State St., Suite 1009
Erie, PA 16501
814–871–4371
Fax: 814–871–4848

Harrisburg Regional Office –
Bureau of Consumer Protection
Office of Attorney General
301 Chestnut St., Suite 105
Harrisburg, PA 17101
717–787–7109
Fax: 717–772–3560

Philadelphia Regional Office –
Bureau of Consumer Protection
Office of Attorney General
21 South 12th St., 2nd Floor
Philadelphia, PA 19107
215–560–2414
Fax: 215–560–2494

Pittsburgh Regional Office –
Bureau of Consumer Protection
Office of Attorney General
Manor Building, 6th Floor
564 Forbes Ave.
Pittsburgh, PA 15219

412–565–5135
Fax: 412–880–0196

Scranton Regional Office –
Bureau of Consumer
Protection
Office of Attorney General
100 Samter Building
101 Penn Ave.
Scranton, PA 18503
570–963–4913
Fax: 570–963–3418

State Banking Authorities
Department of Banking
333 Market St.
16th Floor
Harrisburg, PA 17101–2290
717–787–6991
Toll free in PA: 1–800–PA–
BANKS
TDD toll free: 1–800–679–5070
Fax: 717–787–8773
www.banking.state.pa.us

State Insurance Regulators
Bureau of Consumer Service
Insurance Department
1321 Strawberry Square
13th Floor
Harrisburg, PA 17120
717–787–2317
Toll free: 1–877–881–6388
Fax: 717–787–8585
www.insurance.state.pa.us

State Securities Administrators
Securities Commission
ATTN: Office of Secretary
Eastgate Office Building
2nd Floor
1010 North 7th St.
Harrisburg, PA 17102–1410
717–787–8061
Toll free in PA: 1–800–600–0007
Fax: Fax: 717–783–5122
www.psc.state.pa.us

State Utility Commissions
Public Utility Commission
PO Box 3265
Harrisburg, PA 17105–3265
717–783–7349
Toll free in PA: 1–800–782–1110
Fax: 717–787–5813
puc.paonline.com

Puerto Rico
Department of Justice
PO Box 920192
San Juan, PR 00902
787–721–2900
Fax: 787–725–2475

State Banking Authorities
Department of Financial
Institutions
Fernandez Juncos Station
PO Box 11855
San Juan, PR 009103855

787–723–3131
Fax: 787–723–4042
www.cif.gov.pr

State Insurance Regulators
Office of the Commissioner of
Insurance
Call Box 8330
Fernandez Juncos Station
Santurce, PR 00910–8330
787–722–8686
787–721–5848
Fax: 787–722–4402
www.ocs.gobierno.pr

**State Securities
Administrators**
Office of the Commissioner of
Financial Institutions
Fernandez Juncos Station
PO Box 11855
San Juan, PR 00910–3855
787–723–8403
Fax: 787–723–4225
Email: felipec@cif.gov.pr
www.cif.gov.pr

State Utility Commissions
Public Service Commission
PO Box 190870
San Juan, PR 00919–0817
787–756–1425
Fax: 787–758–3418

Rhode Island
Consumer Protection Unit
Department of Attorney

General
150 South Main St.
Providence, RI 02903
401–274–4400
TDD: 401–453–0410
Fax: 401–222–5110
www.riag.state.ri.us/

State Banking Authorities
Division of Banking
Department of Business
Regulation
233 Richmond St.
Suite 231
Providence, RI 029034231
401–222–2405
TDD/TTY: 401–222–2999
Fax: 401–222–5628
Email:
BankInquiry@dbr.state.ri.us
www.dbr.state.ri.us

State Insurance Regulators
Insurance Division
Department of Business
Regulation
233 Richmond St.
Suite 233
Providence, RI 02903–4233
401–222–2223
TDD: 401–222–2999
Fax: 401–222–5475
www.dbr.state.ri.us

**State Securities
Administrators**

Securities Division
233 Richmond St., Suite 232
Providence, RI 02903–4232
401–222–3048
TDD: 401–222–2999
Fax: 401–222–5629
Email: mpicciri@dbr.state.ri.us
www.dbr.state.ri.us

State Utility Commissions
Public Utilities Commission
89 Jefferson Boulevard
Warwick, RI 02888
401–941–4500
TDD: 401–277–3500
Fax: 401941–4885
www.ripuc.org

South Carolina
State Ombudsman
Office of Executive Policy and
Program
1205 Pendleton St.
Room 308
Columbia, SC 29201
803–734–5049
Toll free in SC: 1–866–300–9333
Fax: 803–734–0799
www.myscgov.com

South Carolina Department of
Consumer Affairs
3600 Forest Drive
Suite 300
PO Box 5757
Columbia, SC 29250

803–734–4200
Toll free in SC: 1–800–922–1594
Fax: 803–734–4286
Email: scdca@dca.state.sc.us
www.scconsumer.gov

Office of the Attorney General
PO Box 11549
Columbia, SC 29211
803–734–3970
Fax: 803–734–4323
Email:
info@scattorneygeneral.com
www.scattorneygeneral.org

State Banking Authorities
State Board of Financial
Institutions
1015 Sumter St., Room 309
Columbia, SC 29201
803–734–2001
Fax: 803–734–2013

State Insurance Regulators
Consumer Services
Department of Insurance
300 Arbor Lake Drive
Suite 1200
P.O. Box 100105
Columbia, SC 29202
803–737–6180
Toll free in SC: 1–800–768–3467
Fax: 803–737–6231
Email:

CnsmMail@doi.state.sc.us
www.doi.state.sc.us

**State Securities
Administrators**
Securities Division
Office of the Attorney General
P. O. Box 11549
Columbia, SC 29211–1549
803–734–9916
www.scsecurities.org/

State Utility Commissions
Office of Regulatory Staff
Consumer Services Dept.
PO Box 11263
Columbia, SC 29211
803–737–5230
Toll free in SC: 1–800–922–
1531
TDD toll free in SC: 1–800–
735–2905
www.regulatorystaff.sc.gov

South Dakota
Consumer Affairs
Office of the Attorney General
State Capitol Building
500 East Capitol
Pierre, SD 57501–5070
605–773–4400
Toll free in SD: 1–800–300–
1986
TDD: 605–773–6585
Fax: 605–773–7163
Email:

consumerhelp@sate.sd.us
www.state.sd.us/atg

State Banking Authorities
Division of Banking
217 1/2 W. Missouri Ave.
Pierre, SD 57501–4590
605–773–3421
Fax: 605–773–5367
www.state.sd.us/banking

State Insurance Regulators
Division of Insurance
Department of Revenue and
Regulation
445 East Capital
Pierre, SD 57501
605–773–3563
Fax: 605–773–5369
www.state.sd.us/drr

**State Securities
Administrators**
Division of Securities
445 East Capitol Ave.
Pierre, SD 57501–3185
605–773–4823
Fax: 605–773–5953
www.state.sd.us/dcr/securitie
s

State Utility Commissions
Public Utilities Commission
Consumer Affairs
500 East Capitol Ave.
Pierre, SD 57501–5070
605–773–3201

Toll free: 1–800–332–1782
(consumer affairs only)
Fax: 605–773–3809
www.state.sd.us/puc/puc.htm

Tennessee
Consumer Advocate and
Protection Division
Office of the Attorney General
PO Box 20207
Nashville, TN 37202–02071
615–741–1671
Fax: 615–532–2910
attorneygeneral.state.tn.us/cpr
o/cpro

Division of Consumer Affairs
500 James Robertson Pkwy.,
5th Floor
Nashville, TN 37243–0600
615–741–4737
Toll free in TN: 1–800–342–
8385
Fax: 615–532–4994
Email:
consumer.affairs@state.tn.us
www.state.tn.us/consumer

State Banking Authorities
Department of Financial
Institutions
The Nashville City Center
511 Union Street, 4th Floor
Nashville, TN 37219
615–253–2023
Toll Free: 1–800–778–4215

TDD/TTY: 615–253–7794
Email:
TDFI.ConsumerResources@st
ate.tn.us
www.state.tn.us/financialinst/

State Insurance Regulators
Department of Commerce and
Insurance
500 James Robertson Pkwy.,
5th Floor
Nashville, TN 37243–0565
615–741–2241
Toll free in TN: 1–800–342–
4029
Fax: 615–532–6934
www.state.tn.us/commerce

**State Securities
Administrators**
Securities Division
Department of Commerce and
Insurance
Davy Crockett Tower, Suite
680
500 James Robertson Pkwy.
Nashville, TN 37243
615–741–2947/615–741–5900
Toll free in TN: 1–800–863–
9117
www.state.tn.us/commerce/

State Utility Commissions
Tennessee Regulatory
Authority
460 James Robertson Pkwy.
Nashville, TN 37243–0505

189

615–741–8953
Toll free: 1–800–342–8359
TDD/TTY toll free: 1–888–276–0677
Fax: 615–741–5015
www.state.tn.us/tra

Texas
Regional Offices
Austin Regional Office
PO Box 12548
Austin, TX 78711–2548
512–463–2185
Toll free: 1–800–621–0508
Fax: 512–473–8301
Email: cac@oag.state.tx.us
www.oag.state.tx.us

Dallas Regional Office
Office of the Attorney General
1600 Pacific Ave., Suite 1700
Dallas, TX 75201–3513
214–969–5310
Fax: 214–969–7615
Email: cac@oag.state.tx.us
www.oag.state.tx.us

El Paso Regional Office
Office of the Attorney General
401 East Franklin St., Suite 530
El Paso, TX 79901
915–834–5800
Fax: 915–592–1546
Email: cac@oag.state.tx.us
www.oag.state.tx.us

Houston Regional Office –
Consumer Protection
Office of the Attorney General
808 Travis, Suite 300
Houston, TX 77002
713–223–5886
Fax: 713–223–5821
Email: cac@oag.state.tx.us
www.oag.state.tx.us

Lubbock Regional Office
Office of the Attorney General
4630 50th Street, Suite 500
Lubbock, TX 79414–3520
806–747–5238/Fax: 806–747–6307
Email: cac@oag.state.tx.us
www.oag.state.tx.us

McAllen Regional Office
Office of the Attorney General
3201 North McColl Road,
Suite B
McAllen, TX 78501–1685
956–682–4547/Fax: 956–682–1957
Email: cac@oag.state.tx.us
www.oag.state.tx.us

San Antonio Regional Office
Office of the Attorney General
115 East Travis St.
Suite 925
San Antonio, TX 78205–1605
210–224–1007
Fax: 210–225–1075

Email: cac@oag.state.tx.us
www.oag.state.tx.us

County Offices

Harris County Consumer
Fraud Division
District Attorney's Office
1201 Franklin
Suite 600
Houston, TX 77002–1923
713–755–5836
Fax: 713–755–5262

State Banking Authorities

Department of Banking
2601 North Lamar
Austin, TX 78705
512–475–1300
Toll free in TX: 1–877–276–5554
Fax: 512–475–1313
www.banking.state.tx.us

State Insurance Regulators

Department of Insurance
333 Guadalupe St.
P.O. Box 149104
Austin, TX 78614–9104
512–463–6169
Toll free in TX: 1–800–252–3439 (consumer help line)
Fax: 512–475–2005
Email:
rbordelon@opic.state.tx.us
www.tdi.state.tx.us

State Securities Administrators

State Securities Board
PO Box 13167
Austin, TX 78711–3167
512–305–8300
Fax: 512–305–8310
www.ssb.state.tx.us

State Utility Commissions

Public Utility Commission
1701 North Congress Ave.
P.O. Box 13326
Austin, TX 78711–3326
512–936–7000
Toll free: 1–888–PUC–TIPS
(782–8477)
TDD/TTY: 512–9367136
Fax: 512–936–7003
Email:
customer@puc.state.tx.us
www.puc.state.tx.us

Utah

Division of Consumer
Protection
Department of Commerce
160 East 300 South, Box
146704
Salt Lake City, UT 84114–6704
801–530–6601
Fax: 801–530–6001
Email:
consumerproection@utah.gov
www.consumerprotection.utah.gov

State Banking Authorities
Department of Financial
Institutions
PO Box 146800
Salt Lake City, UT 84114–6800
801–538–8830
Fax: 801–538–8894
www.dfi.utah.gov

State Insurance Regulators
Department of Insurance
State Office Bldg., Room 3110
Salt Lake City, UT 841146901
801–538–3805
Toll free in UT: 1–800–439–
3805
TDD: 801–538–3826
Fax: 801–538–3829
www.insurance.state.ut.us

**State Securities
Administrators**
Division of Securities
Department of Commerce
160 East 300 South, 2nd Floor
(84111)
PO Box 146760
Salt Lake City, UT 84114–6760
801–530–6600
Toll free in UT: 1–800–721–
7233
Fax: 801–530–6980
www.commerce.state.ut.us

State Utility Commissions
Public Service Commission
160 East 300 South

Salt Lake City, UT 84111
801–530–6716
Toll free in UT: 1–800–874–
0904
TDD: 801–530–6716
Fax: 801–530–6796
Email: psccal@utah.gov
www.psc.state.ut.us

Vermont
Consumer Assistance
Program
Office of the Attorney General
206 Morrill Hall, UVM
Burlington, VT 05405
802–656–3183
Toll free in VT: 1–800–649–
2424
TTY: 802 828–3665
Fax: 802–656–1423
Email: consumer@uvm.edu
www.atg.state.vt.us

Consumer Assurance Section
Food Safety and Consumer
Assurance Division
Agency of Agriculture
116 State St.
Montpelier, VT 05620–2901
802–828–2436
Fax: 802–828–5983

State Banking Authorities
Department of Banking,
Insurance, Securities and
Health Care Administration
89 Main St., Drawer 20

Montpelier, VT 05620–3101
802–828–4872/802–828–3307
(Banking)
Toll free: 1–800–964–1764 (All
insurance except health)
Toll free: 1–800–631–7788
(Health Care)
Fax: 802–828–3306
Email:
rmcNaughton@bishca.state.vt.
us
www.bishca.state.vt.us

State Insurance Regulators
Department of Banking,
Insurance, Securities and
Health Care Administration
89 Main St.
Drawer 20
Montpelier, VT 05620–3101
802–828–3302
Toll free in VT: 1–800–964–
1784
Toll free in VT: 1–800–631–
7788 (Health Insurance)
Fax: 802–828–3306
www.bishca.state.vt.us

**State Securities
Administrators**
Department of Banking,
Insurance, Securities, &
Health Care Administration
89 Main St., Drawer 20
Montpelier, VT 05620–3101
802–828–3420

Fax: 802–828–2896
www.bishca.state.vt.us

State Utility Commissions
Public Service Board
112 State St., Drawer 20
Montpelier, VT 05620–2701
802–828–2358
TDD toll free in VT: 1–800–
253–0191
Fax: 802–828–3351
Email: clerk@psb.state.vt.us
www.state.vt.us/psb

Virginia
Attorney General
Antitrust and Consumer
Litigation Section
Office of the Attorney General
900 East Main St.
Richmond, VA 23219
804–786–2116
Toll free: 1–800–451–1525
Fax: 804–786–0122
Email: mail@oag.state.va.us
www.oag.state.va.us

Office of Consumer Affairs
Department of Agriculture
and Consumer Services
P.O. Box 1163
Richmond, VA 23218
804–786–2042
Toll free in VA: 1–800–552–
9963
TDD toll free: 1–800–828–1120

Fax: 804–225–2666
www.vdacs.state.va.us

County Offices
Consumer Affairs Office
One Court Home Plaza
Suite 302
2100 Clarendon Blvd.
Arlington, VA 22201
703–228–3260/Fax: 703–228–3295
Email: mgray@arlingtonva.us
www.arlingtonva.us

Fairfax County Department of
Cable Communications and
Consumer Protection
12000 Government Center
Parkway
Suite 433
Fairfax, VA 22035
703–222–8435 (Complaints)
703–324–8484 (Consumer
Services)
Fax: 703–322–9542

State Banking Authorities
Bureau of Financial
Institutions
1300 East Main St.
Suite 800
P.O. Box 640
Richmond, VA 23218–0640
804–371–9657
Toll free in VA: 1–800–552–7945
TDD: 804–371–9206

Fax: 804–371–9416
www.state.va.us/scc

State Insurance Regulators
Bureau of Insurance
State Corporation
Commission
PO Box 1157
1300 East Main St. (23219)
(only for special delivery and
walk–ins)
Richmond, VA 23218
804–371–9967
Toll free in VA: 1–800–552–7945
TDD: 804–371–9206
Email:
bureauofinsurance@scc.state.va.us
www.state.va.us/scc

State Securities Administrators
Division of Securities and
Retail Franchising
State Corporation
Commission
PO Box 1197
Richmond, VA 23218
804–371–9051
Toll free in VA: 1–800–552–7945
TDD: 804–371–9203
Fax: 804–371–9911
www.state.va.us/scc/division/srf

State Utility Commissions
State Corporation
Commission
PO Box 1197
Richmond, VA 23218
804-371-9967
Toll free in VA: 1-800-552-7945
TDD: 804-371-9206
Fax: 804-371-9211
www.state.va.us/scc

U.S. Virgin Islands
Department of Licensing and
Consumer Affairs
Golden Rock Shopping Center
Christiansted
St. Croix, VI 00820
340-773-2226
Fax: 340-778-8250
wwww.dlca.gov.vi

State Offices
Department of Licensing and
Consumer Affairs
Property and Procurement
Bldg.
No. 1 Sub Base
Room 205
St. Thomas, VI 00802
340-774-3130
Fax: 340-776-0675
www.dlca.gov.vi

State Banking Authorities
Chairman of Banking Board
Kongen's Gade #18

Charlotte Amalie
St. Thomas, VI 00802
340-774-2991
Fax: 340-774-6953

State Insurance Regulators
Division of Banking and
Insurance
Kongen's Gade #18
St. Thomas, VI 00802
340-774-7166
Fax: 340-774-9458
Email: vidoi001@aol.com

Washington
Office of the Attorney General
(see Regional Consumer
Resource Centers)
1125 Washington St. SE
Olympia, WA 98504-0100
Toll free: 1-800-551-4636
www.atg.wa.gov/

Regional Offices
Bellingham Consumer
Resource Center (Island, San
Juan, Skagit and Whatcom
Counties)
Office of the Attorney General
103 East Holly St., Suite 308
Bellingham, WA 98225-4728
360-738-6185
Toll free in WA: 1-800-551-4636
Fax: 360-738-6190
www.atg.wa.gov

Kennewick Consumer
Resource Center (Southeast
Washington)
Office of the Attorney General
500 N. Morain St., Suite 1250
Kennewick, WA 99336–2607
509–734–7140
Toll free in WA: 1–800–551–4636
Fax: 509–734–7475
www.atg.wa.gov

Seattle Consumer Resource
Center (King, Snohomish,
Clallam and Jefferson
Counties)
Office of the Attorney General
900 Fourth Ave., Suite 2000
Seattle, WA 98164–1012
206–464–6684
Toll free in WA: 1–800–551–4636
Fax: 206–464–6451
www.atg.wa.gov

Spokane Consumer Resource
Center (Northeast
Washington)
Office of the Attorney General
1116 West Riverside Ave.
Spokane, WA 99201–1194
509–456–3123
Toll free in WA: 1–800–551–4636
Fax: 509–458–3548
www.atg.wa.gov

Tacoma Consumer Resource
Center (Pierce, Mason, Grays
Harbor and Kitsap Counties)
Consumer Protection Division
Office of the Attorney General
PO Box 2317
Tacoma, WA 98401
253–593–2904
Toll free in WA: 1–800–551–4636
Fax: 253–593–2449
Email: cynthial@atg.wa.gov
www.atg.wa.gov

Vancouver Consumer
Resource Center (Southwest
Washington)
Office of the Attorney General
1220 Main St.
Suite 549
Vancouver, WA 98660–2964
360–759–2150
Toll free in WA: 1–800–551–4636
Fax: 360–759–2159
www.atg.wa.gov

State Banking Authorities
Department of Financial
Institutions
PO Box 41200
Olympia, WA 98504–1200
360–902–8700
Toll free: 1–877–RING–DFI
Fax: 360–586–5068
www.dfi.wa.gov

State Insurance Regulators
Office of the Commissioner of Insurance
Insurance 5000 Building
P.O. Box 40255
Olympia, WA 98504–0255
360–725–7103
Toll free in WA: 1–800–562–6900
TDD: 360–586–0241
Fax: 360–586–3109
Email: mikek@olc–wa–gov
www.insurance.wa.gov

State Securities Administrators
Securities Division
Department of Financial Institutions
PO Box 9033
Olympia, WA 98507–9033
360–902–8760
TDD: 360–664–8126
Fax: 360–586–5068
www.dfi.wa.gov

State Utility Commissions
Utilities and Transportation Commission
1300 S. Evergreen Park Dr., SW
Olympia, WA 98504
360–664–1173
Toll free in WA: 1–800–562–6150
TTY: 360–586–8203/Fax: 360–586–1150
www.wutc.wa.gov

West Virginia
Consumer Protection Division
Office of the Attorney General
812 Quarrier St.
6th Floor
P.O. Box 1789
Charleston, WV 25326–1789
304–558–8986
Toll free in WV: 1–800–368–8808
Fax: 304–558–0184
Email: consumer@wvago.gov
www.wvago.us

State Banking Authorities
Division of Banking
State Capitol Complex – Building 3
Room 311
1900 Kanawha Blvd. East
Charleston, WV 25305–0240
304–558–2294
Toll free in WV: 1–800–642–9056
Fax: 304–558–0442
www.wvdob.org

State Insurance Regulators
Department of Insurance
1124 Smith St. (25301)
P.O. Box 50540
Charleston, WV 25305–0540
304–558–3354
Toll free in WV: 1–888–TRY–

WVIC (888–879–9842)
Fax: 304–558–0412
Email:
wvins@wvinsurance.gov
www.wvinsurance.gov

State Securities Administrators
Securities Commission
State Auditor's Office
102 Dee Dr.
Charleston, WV 25311
304–558–2257
Toll free: 1–888–368–9507
Fax: 304–558–4211
Email:
securities@wvauditor.com
www.wvauditor.com

State Utility Commissions
Public Service Commission
201 Brooks St.
Charleston, WV 25301
304–340–0300
Toll free in WV: 1–800–344–5113
Fax: 304–340–0325
www.psc.state.wv.us/

Wisconsin
Department of Agriculture, Trade and Consumer Protection
2811 Agriculture Dr.
PO Box 8911
Madison, WI 53708–8911

608–224–4949
Toll free in WI: 1–800–422–7128
TDD: 608–224–5058
Fax: 608–224–4939
Email:
hotline@datcp.state.wi.us
www.datcp.state.wi.us

Regional Offices
Bureau of Consumer Protection
Dept. of Agriculture, Trade & Consumer Protection
200 North Jefferson St., Suite 146A
Green Bay, WI 54301
920–448–5110
Fax: 920–448–5118
Email:
datcphotline@datcp.state.wi.us

Bureau of Consumer Protection
Dept. of Agriculture, Trade and Consumer Protection
10930 West Potter Rd., Suite C
Milwaukee, WI 53226–3450
414–266–1231

County Offices
Racine County Sheriff's Department
717 Wisconsin Ave.
Racine, WI 53403

262–636–3126
Fax: 262–637–5279

State Banking Authorities
Department of Financial
Institutions
345 West Washington Ave.
3rd Floor
Madison, WI 53708
608–264–7969
Toll free in WI: 1–800–452–
3328
Fax: 608–264–7968
www.wdfi.org

State Insurance Regulators
Office of the Commissioner of
Insurance
125 S. Webster St. (53702)
P.O. Box 7873
Madison, WI 53707–7873
608–266–0103
Toll free in WI: 1–800–236–
8517
Dial 711 and ask for 608–266–
3586
Fax: 608–266–9935
Email:
information@oci.state.wi.us
oci.wi.gov

**State Securities
Administrators**
Division of Securities
Department of Financial
Institutions
PO Box 1768

Madison, WI 53701–1768
608–266–1064
Toll free in WI: 1–800–47–
CHECK
TTY: 608–266–8818
Fax: 608–264–7979
www.wdfi.org

State Utility Commissions
Public Service Commission
Consumer Affairs Unit
610 North Whitney Way
(53705)
P.O. Box 7854
Madison, WI 53707–7854
608–266–2001
Toll free: 1–800–225–7729
TDD: 608–267–1479
Fax: 608–266–3957
Email:
jackie.reynolds@psc.state.wi.u
s
psc.wi.gov

Wyoming
Consumer Protection Unit
Office of the Attorney General
123 State Capitol Building
Cheyenne, WY 82002
307–777–7874
Toll free in WY: 1–800–438–
5799
Fax: 307–777–7956
Email:

agwebmaster@state.wy.us
attorneygeneral.state.wy.us

State Banking Authorities
Division of Banking
Herschler Bldg.
3rd Floor, East
Cheyenne, WY 82002
307–777–7797
Fax: 307–777–3555
Email:
maitchison@wyaudit.state.wy.
us
audit.state.wy.us/banking
locklo
State Insurance Regulators
Department of Insurance
Herschler Bldg.,122 West 25th
St.
3rd Floor East
Cheyenne, WY 82002–0440
307–777–7401
Toll free in WY: 1–800–438–
5768
Fax: 307–777–5895
Email: wyinsdep@state.wy.us
insurance.state.wy.us/

**State Securities
Administrators**
Securities Division
Office of the Secretary of State
State Capitol Bldg., Room 109
200 West 24th St.
Cheyenne, WY 82002–0020
307–777–7370
TDD: 307–777–5351

Fax: 307–777–5339
Email: securities@state.wy.us
soswy.state.wy.us

State Utility Commissions
Public Service Commission
2515 Warren Ave., Suite 300
Cheyenne, WY 82002
307–777–7427
Toll free in WY: 1–888–570–
9905
TTY: 307–777–7427
Fax: 307–777–5700
psc.state.wy.us

Appendix B – Monthly Budget Worksheet

This worksheet is used to calculate your total monthly expenses (money going out).

Monthly Expense	Amount
1. Mortgage/Rent	
2. Groceries (food)	
3. Home Insurance	
4. Home Maintenance	
5. Student Loans	
6. Car Payments	
7. Car Maintenance	
8. Car Insurance	
9. Misc Transportation (bus, subway, gas, etc.)	
10. Health insurance	
11. Life insurance	
12. Prescriptions/ Appts	
13. Electricity	
14. Heating (Oil/Gas)	
15. Water/Sewer	
16. Telephone	
17. Cell Phone/Pager	
18. Cable/Satellite TV	
19. Internet Access Fees	
20. Credit Card Payments	
Total Expenses $	

Appendix C – Detailed Monthly Budget Worksheet

This worksheet is used to calculate total money expenses and income to determine if extra money is available after paying all monthly expenses. It can be used for three, six or 12 months at a time.

	Jan	Feb	Mar	Apr
INCOME				
Wages				
Child Support/Alimony/ Other				
TOTAL INCOME				
EXPENSES				
Utilities				
Mortgage/Rent				
Home telephone				
Cellular phone/Pager				
Cable/Satellite TV				
Internet Access				
Home repairs				
Home security alarm				
Groceries/Eating Out				
Child care				
Dry cleaning				
Health insurance				
Life insurance				
Prescriptions				
Magazines/Newspapers				
Barber/Spa/Hairdresser				
Clothing				
Gifts/Books				
Vacations				
Movies/Concerts/Clubs				

Movie Rentals/Music				
Gas/Car Wash/Car maintenance				
Car insurance				
Parking/Public Transportation				
Personal Property Tax (car)				
Child care				
Sports Club/Gym fees				
Retirement(401k, Roth IRA)				
Credit Card payments				
Student Loan Payments				
Savings				
Religious organizations				
Charity				
TOTAL EXPENSES				
MONEY LEFT OVER/MONEY NEEDED				

To calculate your monthly budget, add all rows under the **Income** heading to determine your total net monthly income (after taxes) and enter the value in the **TOTAL INCOME** row. Add all rows under the **Expenses** heading to determine your total monthly expenses and enter the value in the **TOTAL EXPENSES** row.

Subtract your total income from your total expenses (Total income – Total expenses = Money left over or Money needed). If you get a negative number identify what areas you need to reduce spending. If you get a positive number see what additional areas you can reduce spendingto reach other financial goals such as starting a purchasing a home.

Appendix D – Statute of Limitations

The statute of limitations for a delinquent debt is the time limit for a creditor to file a lawsuit against a debtor. This period starts when the debtor first becomes delinquent. However, if a statute of limitations has expired on a particular debt this may **not** necessarily prevent a lawsuit from being filed, but the defendant can have the suit dismissed on this basis. Credit cards are generally considered open accounts. Auto loans and other installment agreements are considered written contracts.

State	Promissory Notes	Oral Agreements	Open Accounts	Written Contracts
Alabama	6	6	3	6
Alaska	6	6	6	6
Arizona	5	3	3	6
Arkansas	6	3	3	5
California	4	2	4	4
Colorado	6	6	6	6
Connecticut	6	3	6	6
Delaware	6	3	3	3
Florida	5	4	4	5
Georgia	6	4	4	6
Hawaii	6	6	6	6
Idaho	10	4	4	5
Illinois	6	5	5	10
Indiana	10	6	6	10
Iowa	5	5	5	10
Kansas	5	3	3	5
Kentucky	15	5	5	15
Louisiana	10	10	3	10
Maine	6	6	6	6
Maryland	6	3	3	3
Massachusetts	6	6	6	6
Michigan	6	6	6	6
Minnesota	6	6	6	6
Mississippi	3	3	3	3
Missouri	10	5	5	10
Montana	8	5	5	8

Nebraska	6	4	4	5
Nevada	3	4	4	6
New Hampshire	6	3	3	3
New Jersey	6	6	6	6
New Mexico	6	4	4	6
New York	6	6	6	6
North Carolina	5	3	3	3
North Dakota	6	6	6	6
Ohio	15	6	?	15
Oklahoma	5	3	3	5
Oregon	6	6	6	6
Pennsylvania	4	4	6	6
Puerto Rico	–	–	3	15
Rhode Island	10	15	10	15
South Carolina	3	10	3	10
South Dakota	6	6	6	6
Tennessee	6	6	6	6
Texas	4	4	4	4
Utah	6	4	4	6
Vermont	5	6	6	6
Virginia	6	3	3	5
Virgin Islands (U.S.)	–	3	–	5
Washington	6	3	3	6
Washington D.C.	3	3	3	3
West Virginia	6	5	5	10
Wisconsin	10	6	6	6
Wyoming	10	8	8	10

Appendix E – Statute of Limitations (Judgments)

After a creditor wins a lawsuit against a debtor and is awarded a judgment by the court, there is a time limit for collecting that judgment. The debtor can also be charged interest on the amount owed for the judgment. However, many states allow judgments to be renewed one or more times, which could significantly extend enforcing the judgment, if the creditor is persistent about the renewals.

State	Statute of Limitations (Years)
Alabama	20
Arkansas	10
Alaska	5
Arizona	10
California	10
Colorado	20
Connecticut	20
Delaware	No Limit
Florida	20
Georgia	7
Hawaii	10
Iowa	6
Idaho	20
Illinois	20
Indiana	20
Kansas	5
Kentucky	15
Louisiana	10
Maine	20
Maryland	12

Massachusetts	20
Michigan	10
Minnesota	10
Mississippi	7
Missouri	10
Montana	10
North Carolina	5
North Dakota	6
Nebraska	20
New Hampshire	20
New Jersey	14
New Mexico	20
Nevada	10
New York	10
Ohio	21
Oklahoma	5
Oregon	10
Pennsylvania	4
Puerto Rico	15
Rhode Island	20
South Carolina	10
South Dakota	20
Tennessee	10
Texas	10
Utah	8
Virginia	8
Vermont	20
Washington	10
Washington D.C.	3
West Virginia	20
Wyoming	5

Appendix F – Credit Report Fees by State

These fees apply if you have already received a copy of your credit report in less than a twelve month time period or if you have not been denied credit in the past sixty days.

State	Credit Report Fee
Alabama	$10.00
Alaska	$10.00
Arizona	$10.00
Arkansas	$10.00
California	$8.00
Colorado	$8.00
Connecticut	$7.95
Delaware	$10.00
Florida	$10.00
Georgia	2 free/ year, then $10
Hawaii	$10.40
Idaho	$10.00
Illinois	$10.00
Indiana	$10.00
Iowa	$10.00
Kansas	$10.00
Kentucky	$10.00
Louisiana	$10.00
Maine	$5.00
Maryland	$5.25
Massachusetts	$8.00
Michigan	$10.00
Minnesota	$3.00
Mississippi	$10.00
Missouri	$10.00
Montana	$8.50
Nebraska	$10.00
Nevada	$10.00
New Hampshire	$10.00
New Jersey	$8.00
New Mexico	$10.50

New York	$10.83
North Carolina	$10.00
North Dakota	$10.00
Ohio	$10.00
Oklahoma	$10.00
Oregon	$10.00
Pennsylvania	$10.70
Puerto Rico	$10.00
Rhode Island	$10.00
South Carolina	$10.50
South Dakota	$10.60
Tennessee	$10.00
Texas	$10.83
Utah	$10.00
Vermont	$7.50
Virginia	$10.00
Virgin Islands (U.S.)	$10.00
Washington	$10.00
Washington D.C.	$10.58
West Virginia	$10.60
Wisconsin	$10.00
Wyoming	$10.00

Resources

Listed below are several companies and organizations that you may contact to receive advice on how to deal with telemarketers, where to file complaints against creditors, and information about your credit rights. These organizations can help you learn about and exercise your credit rights as a consumer.

Bankrate, www.bankrate.com, 561-630-2400, provides rate comparisons, articles and various information on credit cards, mortgages, investments, and money management.

Better Business Bureau (BBB), www.bbb.org, 703-276-0100, contact your local office to file a complaint against a company.

Consumer Action Division, www.consumeraction.gov, 202-501-1794, provides various information for consumers who have a problem with a creditor or other company.

Direct Marketing Association (DMA), www.dmachoice.org/consumerassistance.php, 888–5OPTOUT (888–567–8688), to remove your name from junk mailing lists and phone lists.

Equifax, www.equifax.com, 800–685–1111, credit reporting agency.
Experian, www.experian.com, 888–397–3742, credit reporting agency.

FCRA, www.ftc.gov/os/statutes/fcradoc.pdf – this is federal credit reporting act that protects consumers with credit.

FDCPA, www.ftc.gov/bcp/edu/pubs/consumer/credit/cre27.pdf – this is the fair and debt collection practices act that identifies rights for consumers dealing with creditors.

Federal Communications Commission – www.fcc.gov, 888–CALL–FCC, speak with one of the Consumer and Mediation Specialists to file a complaint regarding telemarketers or debt collectors.

Federal Trade Commission – www.ftc.gov, 877–382–4357, Credit Practices Division, Washington, DC 20580 or contact the state or local office to file a complaint regarding your credit.

TransUnion Fraud Victim Assistance Division, www.transunion.com, 800-680-7289, P.O. Box 6790, Fullerton, CA 92634, provides information on identity theft.

Identity theft websites to get information to help you protect and monitor your personal information to reduce your chances of being a victim of identity theft:

- www.consumer.gov/idtheft
- www.myfico.com/CreditEducation/IDTheft.aspx?fire=2
- www.usps.com/postalinspectors/idthft_ncpw.htm
- www.treas.gov/offices/domestic-finance/financial-institution/cip/identity-theft.shtml.

Privacy Rights Clearinghouse, http://www.privacyrights.org, 619-298–3396, provides information on privacy rights.

Social Security Administration Fraud Hot Line, www.ssa.gov, 800–

269–0271, P.O. Box 17768, Baltimore, MD 21235 if you are a victim of identity theft.

Statute of Limitations, www.naag.org, check with your State Attorney General's Office at to determine when a debt is considered to old to collect in your state.

TransUnion, www.transunion.com, 800–916–8800, credit reporting agency.

Bibliography

All About Credit: Questions And Answers About the Most Common
     Credit Problems, by Deborah McNaughton.

Debt and Saving Money on Interest Payments, by Scott Bilker.

9 Steps to Financial Freedom, by Suze Orman.

Protecting Your Financial Future, by Lee & Kristy Phililps.

Spend Rich Live Well, by Michelle Singletary.

The Automatic Millionaire, by David Bach.

The Total Money Makeover, by Dave Ramsey.

What Every Credit Card User Needs to Know, by Howard Strong.

Zero Debt, by Lynnette Khalfani.

Glossary

Listed below is a glossary of terms that you may hear or see in letters you receive from a creditor that may help you in understanding and repairing your credit.

Adjusted balance – a method where creditors take the amount owed at the start of the billing cycle and subtract any payments made during that billing cycle to compute the finance charge, new purchases are not included.

Alimony – an order by the court to pay money to a former spouse after a divorce.

Annual Percentage Rate (APR) – amount of interest calculated that is paid yearly on a credit card or credit account.

Annual Fee – a yearly amount charged by a credit card company for using its credit card.

Asset – property or money that a person owns.

Authorized User – a person who is listed as having permission to use an account but has no legal responsibility for usage.

Automated Teller Machine (ATM) – a standalone machine that allows a person to retrieve money from a bank account.

Average Daily Balance (ADB) – a method where creditors add your balances for each day in the billing cycle and then divides that total by the number of days in the billing cycle to compute the finance charge. Payments made during the billing cycle are subtracted to get the daily amounts and depending on the creditor, new purchases may or may not be included and is the most common method used by creditors.

Balance – an amount of money owed to a creditor, lender or other company.

Bankruptcy – when a debtor files a petition with the court claiming that they are unable to pay the creditors owed and a court decides that the debtor is legally unable to pay their debts which is approved as a Chapter 7 or Chapter 13 bankruptcy.

Billing Cycle – the time elapsed between billing periods for goods sold or services rendered, which is usually a month.

Billing Period – the time elapsed between billing periods for goods sold or services rendered, which is usually a month.

Budget – a calculated list of money a person earns as well as the amount of money owed to creditors or lenders over a specific period of time plus estimated expenses.

Budget Counselor – a person or company that helps a person create a budget and learn how to manage their money effectively to prevent serious debt or bankruptcy.

Certificate of Deposit (CD) – a type of deposit account with a bank that typically offers a higher rate of interest than a regular savings account and is insured up to $100,000. When a CD is purchased, you invest a fixed sum of money for a fixed period of time, such as six months, one year or five years, and the bank pays you interest. When you cash in your CD you receive the money you originally invested plus any accrued interest.

Certified Public Accountant (CPA) – a financial advisor that can assist companies and individuals to achieve various financial goals and remain in compliance with various state and federal laws.

Charge Off – an account that becomes delinquent and the creditor writes the debt off as a loss for tax purposes and can continue to collect the debt by selling it or sending it to a collection agency, also referred to as a profit and loss.

Chapter 7 – a type of bankruptcy where all of your assets are sold by a court appointed trustee and the proceeds are distributed to your creditors to pay your debts.

Chapter 13 – a type of bankruptcy where a payment plan is setup to pay back the debts owed to creditors with a total unsecured debt less than $290,525 or secured debt less than $871,550. This type of bankruptcy allows you to keep your property and make regular payments to an account usually over a three to five year period. The repayment ranges from 10 to 100 percent depending on your income and the type of debt owed.

Check Card – a type of credit card that can be used to charge items and is paid by using money available in a bank checking account; the item can be paid by charging the amount to your account or by directly accessing your account and withdrawing the money.

Child Support – a court order to pay money to one parent to financially support a child.

Collection – a delinquent debt that is reported to a third party agency to obtain a debt owed.

Collection Agency – a company that collects a delinquent debt on behalf of a creditor.

Consumer Disclosure – information provided to a potential customer that helps compare credit costs and terms of companies.

Cosign – a person that lends their names and good credit histories to the primary borrower (called the maker). If that person dies, loses a job or otherwise fails to make payments, the cosigner is legally responsible to do so and this information is reporter on the cosigner's credit report.

CRA – an agency that provides credit and collection data on an account holder during a specific time period (usually in years) and compiles this information which can be released in the form of credit reports.

Credit – a form of borrowing money from a person or company and paying the money owed at a later time, usually with interest charged in addition to the money owed.

Credit Agency – an agency that provides credit and collection data on an account holder during a specific time period (usually in years) and compiles this information which can be released in the form of credit reports.

Credit Bureau Agency – an agency that provides credit and collection data on an account holder during a specific time period (usually in years) and compiles this information which can be released in the form of credit reports.

Credit Card – a card that allows you to purchase items on credit paying the money owed at a later time, usually with interest charged in addition to the money owed.

Credit Counseling Agency – a company that advises you on managing your money and debts, helps you develop a budget, and usually offer free educational materials and workshops.

Credit Counselor – a person who works at a credit counseling agency and is qualified to give advice on how to manage outstanding debts.

Credit History – a partial profile of your financial history over a specific period of time, usually in years, which shows your history of paying bills and what is owed for each account.

Credit Limit – the total amount you are authorized to charge on a credit card.

Creditor – a company that loans money to an individual or company who agrees to pay that account based on the terms that company has established.

Credit Repair – the process of reviewing or rebuilding your credit rating to fix incorrect information which increases your chances of being approved for credit or a loan.

Credit Report – a document or report that lists your credit history over a specific period of time (usually in years), and is updated using information obtained from your creditors, lenders, or other companies.

Credit Reporting Agency – an agency that provides credit and collection data on an account holder during a specific time period (usually in years) and compiles this information which can be released in the form of credit reports.

Credit Score – a score developed by the Fair Isaac Corporation that lenders use to rate potential customers in determining the likelihood that a customer will pay their bills on time. They are three types of credit scores, Beacon from Equifax; Empirica from TransUnion and Fair Isaac from Experian.

Debit Card – a type of credit card that can be used to charge items and is paid using money available in a bank account.

Debt – amount of money owed to a company that provides a service, i.e. credit card, loan, etc.

Debt Collector – a collection agency or creditor's collection department or a person who collects debts. This could be: a creditor collecting a debt themselves (this includes people or businesses who have been sold or assigned a debt by the original creditor) or someone acting on behalf of a creditor (i.e. an independent collection agency).

Debt Management – a means of reducing or completely eliminating outstanding debt by managing your money and working with creditors, usually done with the help of a credit or budget counselor.

Debtor – person who owes money to a creditor, lender or other company.

Debt Ratio – the total monthly credit payments divided by your total monthly income, which is used to determine your credit worthiness.

Debt–to–income ratio – the total monthly credit payments divided by your total monthly income, which is used to determine your credit.

Delinquent – a debt that was paid past the monthly due date or a debt that was not paid, a debt that is 30, 60, 90 days or more late.

Department Store Account – a credit card granted by a department store; it can be a 30 day or revolving account.

Divorce Decree – a ruling that summarizes the rights and responsibilities of the divorced parties. A document that states the basic information regarding the divorce, case number, parties, date of divorce, and terms the parties have agreed upon.

Divorcee – a divorced woman.

Equal Credit Opportunity Act – gives women ways to build their own credit history.

Estate – The total of one's possessions, especially all the property and debts left by one at death.

Expenses – money spent for products and services that you purchase.

Fair Credit Reporting Act – provides information for consumers on how to correct mistakes on their credit report.

Fair Isaac Corporation – a company that provides decision making solutions for companies such as banks, credit card issuers, etc.

FCRA – provides information for consumers on how to correct mistakes on their credit report.

FDCPA – provides information on consumer's rights and legal

Federal Debt and Collection Practices Act – provides information on consumer's rights and legal collection practices that creditors must follow.

collection practices that creditors must follow.

FICO – a company that provides decision making solutions for companies such as banks, credit card issuers, etc.

FICO score – a score developed by the Fair Isaac Corporation that lenders use to rate potential customers in determining the likelihood that a customer will pay their bills on time.

Finance Charge – the total cost of a loan or line of credit. The charges include interest, service charges, transaction charges and other fees.

Foreclosure – when a bank takes possession of a property that is delinquent in mortgage payments.

Garnishment – a court order that requires a debtor to pay money for a debt owed to a company that is deducted from the debtor's paycheck until the amount is paid in full.

Gas Card – a credit card that can be used to purchase gas.

Grace Period – time period when a billing cycle ends and the date a bill is due to a creditor to avoid paying finance charges.

Housing and Urban Development - sells foreclosed government homes to individuals or investors.

HUD – Housing and Urban Development, sells foreclosed government homes to individuals or investors.

Identifying information – any personal information that is used to distinguish one person from another such as social security number, address, date of birth, etc.

Identity Theft – when someone other than yourself has obtained your personal information and either accesses or uses your accounts, creates new ones or makes purchases in your name.

Income – money you earn from a job or interest earned on money saved.

Individual Account – an account where only one person uses an account and is legally responsible for making payments.

Inquiry – list of companies who accessed your credit report to review your account or to contact you to extend an offer of credit. These remain on your credit report for two years.

Installment – when a certain amount of money is borrowed and is expected to be repaid in a set period of time for accounts such as mortgage loans, installments loans, etc.

Installment Account – an account where a certain amount of money is borrowed and is expected to be repaid in a set period of time for accounts such as mortgage loans, installments loans, etc.

Interest – an amount of money paid to a creditor or lender for the use of borrowed money.

Interest – an amount of money paid to a creditor or lender for the use of borrowed money.

Interest Rate – the amount of interest charged, usually a percentage of the money borrowed, which is calculated over a specific period of time (usually a year).

Joint Account – an account that two people can use and share legal responsibility for making payments.

Judgment – a court order to pay money to a creditor for a debt owed.

Judgment Proof – a person who has no funds or assets to satisfy a money judgment therefore the creditor cannot collect any money and the judgment is useless.

Lender – a person or entity who loans money to others.

Lien – an official judgment that is recorded in court and county records indicating that a debtor owes a creditor a certain amount of money and attaches the debt to a piece of property so that if the property is sold the debt will be repaid.

Minimum Monthly Payment – the smallest amount of money that can be sent to a creditor to pay on an account to keep it current (usually 4% of the total balance).

Minimum Payment – the smallest amount of money determined by a creditor that can be sent to pay on an account to keep it current (usually 4% of the total balance).

Mortgage – a loan that is used to purchase real estate, which gives the bank an interest in the property until the loan is paid in full.

Negotiate – the process of coming to a resolution or agreement between the creditor and debtor regarding a delinquent debt.

Open Account – a revolving account or line of credit that can be used over and over again such as credit cards, overdraft checking accounts, home equity lines of credit, department store cards or other credit accounts.

Oral Agreement – an unwritten agreement between two or more parties.

Oral Contract – an unwritten agreement between two or more parties.

Previous Balance – a method that creditors use where the amount owed at the start of the billing cycle is used to compute the finance charge.

Probate – claims on real property typically on the estate of a deceased person.

Promissory note – a written promise to pay or repay a specified sum of money at a stated time or on demand.

Public Record – information obtained from state and county courts or collection agencies such as bankruptcies, foreclosures, lawsuits, garnishments, judgments, and liens that is reported on your credit report.

Repossession – this occurs when a creditor seizes a piece of personal property due to a delinquent debt (lack of payment which is usually 90 days or more late).

Revolving Account – an account where a fixed amount of credit that is expected not to be exceeded and where a set amount is expected to be repaid every month for accounts such as credit cards.

Revolving Debt – a fixed amount of credit that is expected not to be exceeded and where a set amount is expected to be repaid every month for accounts such as credit cards.

Secured Credit Card - a credit card where a debtor gives a certain amount of money to the bank to be used as a security, so that if the debtor charges an item and fails to repay, the money can be used to pay for the item.

Secured Debt – amount of money owed to a company that provides a service, i.e. credit card, loan, etc. where the debtor gives a certain amount of money to the bank to be used as security, so that if the debtor charges an item and fails to repay, the money can be used to pay for the item.

Settlement – an agreement that is reached between a debtor and a creditor that satisfies or eliminates a debt.

Spending Plan – a calculated list of money a person earns as well as the amount of money owed to creditors or lenders over a specific period of time plus estimated expenses.

Student Loan – an unsecured loan, used to pay for college that is offered through a bank or loan agency and backed by the government.

Taxes – an amount owed to a federal, state or local government.

Taxing Authority – organizations that are authorized by state statute to levy taxes on real estate and tangible personal property to fund their operations and services as provided by their annual budgets.

Tax Lien – an official judgment that is recorded in court and county records indicating that a debtor owes a taxing authority a certain amount of money and attaches the debt to a property so that if the property is sold the debt will be repaid.

Telemarketer – companies who seek to entice or encourage one to obtain credit or make a purchase.

Travel Account – a fixed amount of credit that is expected to be repaid within 30 days of the billing date, such as American Express, Diners Club cards, or other travel and entertainment cards, sometimes referred to as a 30 day credit account.

Truth in Lending – laws that require creditors to provide information about the cost of buying something on credit or obtaining a loan, this information is called a disclosure and also allows the consumer three days to change their mind about certain credit card transactions that use your home as collateral and limits a consumer's risk on lost or stolen credit cards.

Two Cycle Average Daily Balance – a method where creditors use the average daily balances for two billing cycles to compute the finance charge, payments will be subtracted to get the balances, and new purchases may or may not be included.

Unsecured Credit Card – a credit card where a creditor lends a debtor money and the debtor makes monthly payments to pay the debt owed.

Unsecured Debt – amount of money owed to a company that provides a service, i.e. credit card, loan, etc. where a creditor lends you money and you make monthly payments to pay the debt owed.

Wage Garnishment – a court order that requires a debtor to pay money for a debt owed to a company that is deducted from the debtor's paycheck until the amount is paid in full.

Widow – a woman whose husband has died.

Widower – a man who wife has died.

Writ – a judicial order or a formal written command, issued from the court, requiring the performance of a specific act.

Written Contract – an installment account or loan that is used for a certain period of time with a specified limit.

INDEX

4

401(k), 31, 44, 108

A

account, 18, 19, 23, 24, 30, 31,
32, 33, 34, 35, 37, 38, 39, 41,
44, 45, 46, 52, 53, 54, 55, 59,
62, 63, 65, 68, 70, 71, 75, 78,
85, 87, 88, 89, 92, 93, 94, 95,
98, 102, 109, 111, 114, 115,
116, 132, 134, 136, 138, 214,
215, 216, 217, 218, 219, 220,
222, 223, 224, 226, 227
Account, 220, 222, 224
Adjusted balance, 214
agency, 15, 20, 45, 53, 54, 59,
65, 77, 78, 83, 84, 85, 91, 97,
109, 115, 122, 128, 137, 216,
217, 219, 225
Alimony, 51, 202, 214
American Express, 104, 121,
123, 226, 237
Annual Percentage Rate, 214
APR, 93, 113, 214
Asset, 214
ATM, 33, 133, 214
Attorney, 91, 97, 142, 144, 145,
146, 147, 149, 150, 151, 154,
155, 157, 158, 159, 160, 161,
162, 163, 164, 165, 166, 169,
171, 176, 177, 178, 179, 180,
182, 183, 184, 185, 186, 187,
188, 189, 190, 191, 192, 193,
195, 196, 197, 199, 212
Authorized User, 214

B

bad, 11, 12, 17, 18, 27, 39, 53,
54, 56, 64, 65, 71, 93, 96, 99,
104, 105, 109, 116, 121, 123,
139, 235
Balance, 40, 43, 214, 215, 224
bank, 31, 32, 33, 34, 46, 55, 59,
62, 68, 92, 109, 121, 123, 131,
133, 134, 136, 137, 138, 142,
145, 149, 214, 215, 216, 219,
221, 223, 225, 235
bank account, 219
bankruptcy, 16, 49, 51, 52, 63,
64, 95, 104, 215
Bankruptcy, 49, 52, 215
BBB, 84, 115, 126, 128, 135,
139, 210
Better Business Bureau, 84,
210
Bounced check, 80
budget, 29, 30, 39, 44, 46, 51,
94, 215, 219
Budget, 29, 43, 109, 117, 201,
202, 215
budgeting, 50
bureau, 20, 45, 78, 109
Bureau, 84, 210, 217, 219

C

car loan, 42, 52, 56, 64
card, 12, 14, 15, 19, 25, 27, 33,

229

How to Get out of Debt:
Get an "A" Credit Rating for Free Using the System I've Used Successfully with Thousands of Clients
Consulting

Harrine Freeman solves problems. Why not let her handle your credit repair and money management problems? Email her at hfreeman@hefreemanenterprises.com to schedule an appointment.

"I would like to highly recommend your viewers to purchase this book as I have already referred several clients myself. I can accredit my success and accomplishments to Harrine for not only her service, but her advice as well". – M. Smith (Washington, DC)

How to Get out of Debt: Get an "A" Credit Rating for Free Using the System I've Used Successfully with Thousands of Clients Seminars

If you would like to get more information on how to repair your credit you can attend one of my seminars. You'll get tips on how to find a good bank, setup payment plans, know if a deal is good or bad, and many more topics. Seminars are available in the Washington DC Area but can be arranged for groups of ten or more Nationwide. If you would like to get more details send an email to speakingreq@adeptpublishers.com.

About the Author

Harrine Freeman has a B.S. degree in Computer Science. She has written articles for various financial and self help magazines. She has been a guest speaker at local churches, schools and radio shows. She is a member of the Women Network, NAWW, SPAWN, SPAN, PMA, American Association of Daily Money Managers and Credit Professionals International. Her first book, How to Get out of Debt: Get an "A" Credit Rating for Free Using the System I've Used Successfully with Thousands of Clients was published by Adept Publishers. She currently lives in Washington DC.

How to Get out of Debt: Get an "A" Credit Rating for Free Using the System I've Used Successfully with Thousands of Clients Order Form

Adept Publishers
P.O. Box 60851
Washington, DC 20039
bookorder@adeptpublishers.com

Name: _____

Address: _____

City, State: _____

Zip Code: _____

Email Address: _____

Cost – $19.95 Plus $4.20 shipping and handling

Quantity: _____

Total Amount Enclosed: $_____

Payment: _____ Money Order _____ Check

Credit Card: ___MasterCard ___Visa ___American Express
___ Discover

Card Number: _____

Name as it appears on card: _____

Expiration Date: _____

Please Make Check or Money Orders Payable to: Adept Publishers.